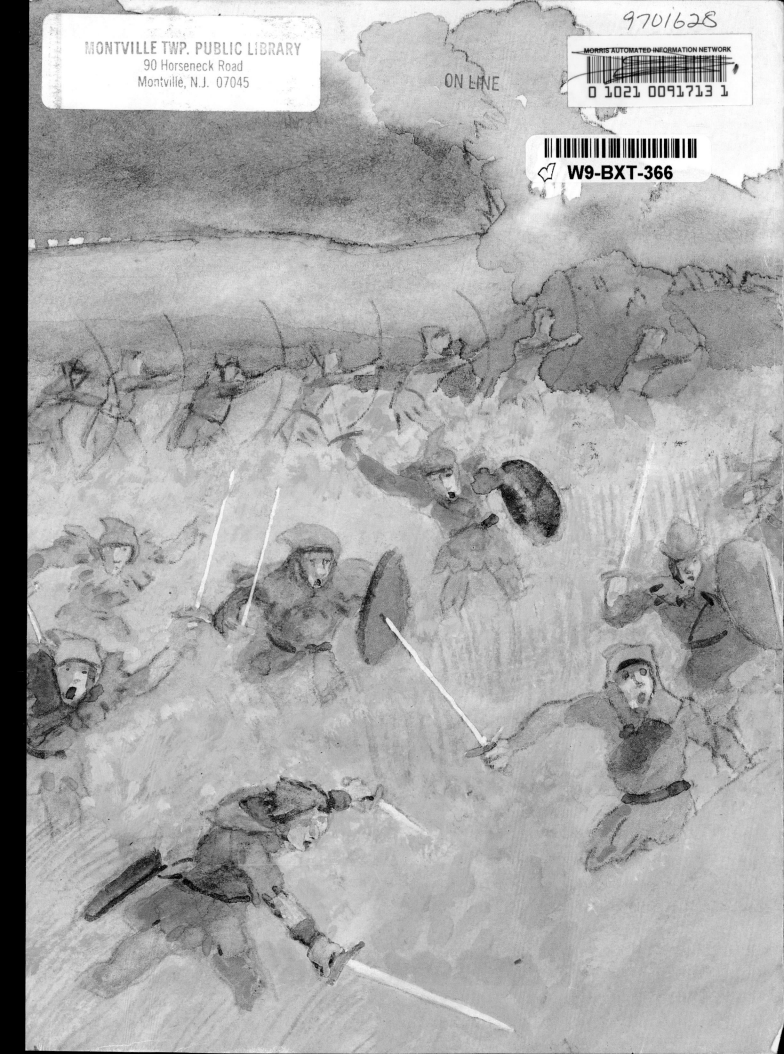

ROBIN
OF SHERWOOD

MICHAEL MORPURGO

ROBIN
OF SHERWOOD

ILLUSTRATED BY
MICHAEL FOREMAN

HARCOURT BRACE & COMPANY
San Diego   New York   London

For Michael and Louise,
Ben and Jack
—M. M.

First published in Great Britain in 1996 by Pavilion Books Limited

Text copyright © 1996 by Michael Morpurgo
Illustrations copyright © 1996 by Michael Foreman

Library of Congress Cataloging-in-Publication Data
Morpurgo, Michael.
Robin of Sherwood/Michael Morpurgo;
illustrated by Michael Foreman.
p. cm.
Companion title to: Arthur, high king of Britain.
Summary: A twelve-year-old boy dreams about the life
and adventures of Robin Hood who lived in Sherwood Forest
as an outlaw dedicated to fighting tyranny.
ISBN 0-15-201315-6
1. Robin Hood (Legendary character)—Legends.
[1. Robin Hood (Legendary character)—Legends.
2. Folklore—England.] I. Foreman, Michael, 1938– ill.
II. Robin Hood (Legend). English. III. Title.
PZ8.1.M8265Ro   1996
398.2—dc20   95-45740

First U.S. edition 1996

Printed in Italy
A C E F D B

CONTENTS

ONE

The LONGEST NIGHT

There had never been a storm like it. The wind roared in from the west one evening in early October. No one was expecting it, least of all the forecasters. The ground, already saturated from a week of continuous rain, could not hold the trees in place. They too had been caught unawares.

I watched all evening long, face pressed up against my bedroom window. Still top-heavy in leaf, the trees were like clippers in full sail caught in a hurricane. They keeled over and could not right themselves. Great branches were torn off like twigs. Roots were wrenched from the earth and towering oaks and beeches sent crashing to the ground. Gran called me from downstairs again and again, but I did not want to leave my window. The trees I loved were being massacred before my eyes, but perversely I could not bear to drag myself away.

In the end Gran came up to my room to fetch me. The safest place, she said, was under the stairs. That was where they had always hidden during the war, when the bombs were falling. Now, as then, the electricity was out. The telephone was out, too. We were on our own and no one could help us. The cupboard under the stairs was a clutter of brooms and vacuums and old tennis rackets, all interlaced with cobwebs. We huddled together, covered ourselves in a musty blanket, and watched the guttering candle.

"We have plenty of candles," she told me, "and plenty of hot tea." She patted a thermos beside her. "We'll be all right. Try and get some sleep now."

But it was to be a sleepless night, and the longest night of my life. The storm lashed the house, rattling doors and shattering windows, shaking the place to its foundations. Both of us very soon gave up any pretense of not being frightened. We clung together as the beast outside roared and raged, doing his worst to destroy the house and us with it. At least, I thought, at least my tree would be safe. It was the biggest in the forest. It took five grown-up people, hands touching, to encircle its massive trunk. No storm in the world could blow it down, not even this one. That thought gave me some comfort through the long night.

When morning came and the beast had gone, we at last dared to venture out. From the kitchen window, most of which had been blown into the sink, we looked out on a scene of utter devastation. The lawn was littered with roof tiles and branches, and the garden shed had been lifted up bodily and smashed against the wall.

Gran sat down slowly at the table and put her hands over her face for a few moments. As she took them away again, I could see she was trying to smile through her tears.

"How about some breakfast?" she said.

"My tree," I told her. "First, I've got to see my tree."

She was not happy for me to go, but I would not be put off. "If you must, then," she said, "but don't be long, and be careful of falling branches. It's still blowing out there."

So off I went, picking my way across the lawn, through the smashed gate, and out into the woods at the back of the house. Most of my twelve years had been spent in this place. Hardly anyone else ever came here—they preferred the flat grass and the football posts of the Rec. But I liked being on my own. This was my refuge and my private paradise. Now as I walked, I saw about me a landscape laid waste. The trees lay like fallen soldiers, mown down in crowded ranks. There were

a few left upright, but some of those were still standing only because they were propped up by others.

A roe deer was drinking at the stream. He should have sprung away, startled at my approach. Instead he glanced almost casually toward me, considered me for a moment, and wandered off in a daze of bewilderment. A squirrel sat not more than a few feet from me, soaked and trembling. I leaped the swollen stream at its narrowest and began to climb the hill on the other side, hoping against hope that when I reached the top I would look down and find my tree still standing—that by some miracle it had survived the holocaust. But as I looked around me now, I knew that neither its size nor its age nor its great strength would have helped it through the night. For the most part, the young, whippy trees seemed to have outlasted many of the oldest trees. And when at last I made it up that blasted hillside and stood there on the ridge, I saw my tree stretched out on its side like a slain giant, its massive roots ripped from the ground.

"No! No!" I cried, and a flock of crows lifted off its crippled branches and were blown away by the wind.

A tree just dead feels the same as a live one. I put my arms around it and laid my cheek on its wrinkled bark. I ran my hands along its trunk and climbed in

among the branches, where I had hidden so often, where I had watched badgers playing in the gathering dusk or foxes pouncing on early worms—where I had been able to sit and look out over the whole forest and feel I was a bird among birds.

I clambered down into the vast crater and looked up. I felt the sun on the back of my head and shivered. At that moment a clod of earth parted from the roots above me and came crashing down at my feet, where it shattered into pieces.

There was something in the debris too solid and too shaped to be just earth. I bent down and picked it up. I was right. I knocked off the earth still clinging to it and rubbed it on my coat. It was sharpened to a point, like an arrowhead, and appeared to be made of some kind of a metal.

I turned it over in my hand and examined it more closely. It *was* an arrowhead.

I sat down on a rock halfway up the side of the crater. I had to study the arrowhead to be quite sure that it was what it seemed to be. I decided it could be nothing else. I sneezed suddenly, violently, and dropped it. When I bent to pick it up, I saw something protruding from the earth, like a torn root, yet too smooth to be a root. I pulled at it and it came away easily. It was a horn, a cow's horn perhaps, blackened by age, and huge. I knocked the earth out of it and found that it was hollow all the way up.

I looked around me for more, not knowing at all what to expect, only that I expected to find something. It was then that I noticed, only a few feet away from me, the shape of a head in the earth, a raised rib cage below it, and then an unmistakable foot.

I hesitated, fearful of what else I would find. If this was what I suspected it to be, then perhaps it should not be disturbed. But I had to know. I brushed away the earth. There were two feet now, and something else that looked like a long curved stick. I drew it out, wiped it, and laid it on the ground alongside the cow's horn. I dug deeper now, my fingers scooping away at the earth. The skull, if that was what it was, was looking away from me down into the crater. I did not want to pick it up, but I had to be sure.

If there were holes for eyes, then I would know for certain. I reached down and lifted it. As I did so the earth fell away and the eyes stared back at me, empty. I shuddered and dropped it at once. It rolled away from me and came to rest at the bottom of the crater, the eyes still staring, accusing. My legs felt suddenly weak. I went to sit down on the rock and considered the grave I had disturbed. I knew then that I had defiled it, that I should have left it alone.

I had fainted in the past—always before breakfast, as it was now. I felt the swoon coming over me and gripped the arrowhead in my hand as tightly as I could, making it hurt me, anything to keep my head from spinning. I tried to think only of the pain, but then I could not feel it anymore. I saw the crows wheeling overhead, buffeted by the wind, and I hoped they would not take me for a dead sheep and peck my eyes out. The rushing clouds rained leaves on me, black leaves that flapped and cawed and covered the sun, so that the world of darkness closed in on me and swirled me away.

TWO

The KING'S DEER

 It was the same dream, always the same dream. Knowing it was a dream—and Robin always seemed to know it, even when he was in it—made it no less terrifying for him. And this time Robin promised himself he would dream his dream right to the bitter end, and remember it. He would force himself to remember it. Somehow he knew that this dream foretold his own death, a death he might still avoid if only he could remember it this time.

The boy in his dream moved through the stricken forest as if in a daze. He was weeping silent tears as he walked. He seemed to be looking for something in particular among the debris of the forest. Then he saw it, cried out, and ran down the hill. The biggest tree in the forest lay dead, its great branches crushed and twisted and torn. The boy put his arms around its trunk and laid his cheek on it. He clung to it as if he would never let go.

The boy was dressed like no one Robin had ever seen before. He wore a hooded green coat trimmed with fur, and pale blue trousers now covered in mud. And his hair was white, snow white.

He was whispering to the tree, and then he was clambering down into the crater left by the roots. A clod of earth landed at his feet. He bent down and picked something up. He cleaned off the earth and rubbed the object on his coat. He turned it over in his hand and then went to sit down on a rock. When the boy rubbed it on his coat a second time, he saw clearly that he had found an arrowhead—Robin seemed to know before the boy did. It gleamed a dull silver in the pale morning sun.

Still Robin dreamed on, dreading how his dream might end. He knew what would happen next, though. The boy found the hunting horn first, and then the bow, which was as big as Robin's father's. Then he saw the bones.

The boy crouched down, digging away the earth with his hands, his eyes wide with fear. Then the boy was reaching out, reaching down toward Robin. He was taking him by the back of his head and lifting the corpse.

Someone was lifting him—Father perhaps. Robin would wake now and stop the dream, before it went any further. Enough was enough. He did not want to have to go on.

Robin tried not to look at the skull. He looked instead at the boy holding the skull and saw himself, as he always did. He had always thought the boy in the dream was himself; but now he was not quite so sure. He was older than this boy, a lot older, and he did not have white hair. His hair was black, black as charcoal. He had dreamed this much before but no more. This time he would not wake up, in spite of Father calling him and shaking him. This time he would finish, finish and remember and exorcise.

The boy dropped the skull back into the earth. It rolled into the bottom of the crater, rolling over and over, until it was still at last, gazing up at the sky and then at the boy.

Now at last Robin knew. Those empty staring eyes were his eyes. He was the skull, but he was the boy, too. He was both. He was the boy sitting on the rock with the arrowhead in his hand, and he was the skull lying in the earth.

He would remember everything now, everything, so that he could save himself. He promised himself all this before he woke; but as he woke, he forgot every single thing he had dreamed.

Robin's father was bending over him, shaking him by the shoulder. "Are you awake, Robin?"

"I was dreaming." Robin sat up, still struggling to remember.

"You can't eat dreams," said his father. "Up you get." And he pulled back the blankets, letting the cold air in.

This was the time of day Robin most missed his mother, remembered her most clearly. There was no warmth of her cheek on his, no whispered welcome to the new day. The last winter had taken her from them. As the autumn leaves fell in the first frost, the Sheriff's men had paid them a visit, Sir Guy of Gisbourne at their head. They had driven off all their pigs, killed the milk cow before their eyes, taken Robin's family's winter's store of corn, and burned down the barn, just for good measure. "Tax collecting," Sir Guy of Gisbourne had called it, and said if the family did not pay up on time next year then the men would be back again. With that, they had ridden off, the forest ringing with their whooping laughter.

The snows had fallen all December, shrouding the forest. Hunting was difficult. Those creatures that could, stayed underground. Those that had to come out to feed moved warily. You cannot tread without being heard against the deep silence of snow; both hunter and prey know as much. There were the deer, of course, but take a deer and you were a dead man. "You bring home a deer, and I'm telling you, I won't touch it," Robin's mother had warned them, and she meant it.

His mother fed him and his father with what little there was and denied herself. They were the hunters; they had to have food—so she reasoned. By the new year she was so weak she was unable to get out of bed in the mornings, too ill even to know or care anymore what her food was. When they brought home a small roe deer, skinned it, and cooked it, they hoped it would revive her. But she was too near death by then even to swallow. Robin and his father ate it together after they had buried her.

Robin's father had spoken little about her dying. But standing over her grave, he had made a promise, a promise that echoed now in Robin's head as he sat sleepy-headed and pulled on his boots: "From this moment I swear I will hunt nothing but the King's deer, and I will feed every hungry soul that lives in this forest. That is my vow. Let them catch me if they can." So for over a year now, father and son had spent their dawns and dusks hunting through the forest, killing the King's deer whenever they found them. Always in the dead of night, and always alone, Robin's father would carry the venison far and wide through the forest, distributing the meat among the starving and the poor. Today would be another such day, and Robin savored the thought of it as he picked up his bow and followed his father out into the cold of the dawn, his breath like smoke in the air.

They never took the same track twice, never moved without listening to the forest. If there were strangers about, the birds told them so, their chorus shrill and agitated. It was too early now for the birds, but Robin and his father knew they were safe enough until first light. The Sheriff's men never dared venture into the forest in the dark, even in numbers. Outcasts killed silently. No one ever saw the Outcasts, but everyone knew they were there, or thought they were. They would cut your throat as soon as look at you, or so it was said. Robin thought he had glimpsed them just once, white hair and red eyes behind a shiver of leaves, but he had not stayed to find out for sure to whom they belonged.

Robin's thoughts were elsewhere now. With his father he always felt safe against anything or anyone, Sheriff's men or Outcasts. His father strode ahead of him now, his great bow slung over his shoulder, the bow Robin could scarcely bend despite his sixteen years.

He might not be able to bend the great bow and he might still have to run to keep up with his father's walk, for he was slight in body and short in leg; but with his own bow he could shoot just as straight as his father, though not as far, perhaps. Before Robin ever tried for his first deer, his father had taught him how to split a wand of willow at fifty paces. "Thumb knuckle to the tip of the nose. A deep breath and hold, but not for too long. Draw a line through the air, arrowhead to target, arch the line for range. Think of the wind. Then will it away."

His father left the first deer that morning to Robin. The young stag was close enough and downwind, barely thirty paces away, standing in the morning mists, his antlered head watching, scenting. Robin let loose, and the arrow followed his line in the air straight to its mark. The stag's legs collapsed under him. He rolled over on his side and lay still. Without thinking, Robin sprinted out of the trees and into the open.

He had gone only a few paces when he was grabbed from behind and hurled to the ground. His father lay beside him, breathing hard, his eyes blazing.

"What's the matter with you, Robin? Haven't I told you? Run in the forest, and you can be heard for miles. Do you want to bring the Sheriff's men down on us? Do you?—And when you've killed, what have I always taught you?"

"Watch and wait," Robin whispered, and his father's grip slackened.

"You'll be the death of me yet, Robin Hood," he said, ruffling Robin's hair and then hauling him to his feet. "That was a fine shot. He died on his feet. By tonight, there'll be a dozen or more people less hungry, and that's something." He took his knife from his belt and handed it to Robin, hilt first. "We'll leave the head for the Sheriff's men as usual; but we have to be quick, it's getting light already."

They had just dropped to their knees beside the dead stag when they heard the snorting. It seemed to come from behind them. There was the sound of leather on leather, the jangle of harness and hushed urgent voices. After that it all happened so fast. One moment they were alone in the clearing with the stag; the next, the ground shook with the thunder of hooves. The Sheriff's men were all around them, and Robin's father was laying about him on all sides with his sword, roaring in his rage.

"Go, Robin! Go while you can!"

Robin looked around him. The soldiers were coming out of the trees from every side, dozens of them, on horseback, on foot. His father was entirely surrounded. There was no reaching him, no helping him.

"Robin, in your mother's name, will you go!"

He ran. He ran like a hare runs, as his father had taught him, weaving, dodging, swerving—and he was fast, too, but not fast enough. He felt a horse pounding behind him, and another was charging directly toward him. He threw the knife, because it was all he could think to do.

It took the rider coming at him in the throat. Robin swerved away, not even looking back to see the man fall, and made for the trees. One glance back now, and Robin saw his father pinioned by his arms, spitting defiance in the face of his captors, the blood running down his face. Then two riders were coming after Robin, swords drawn.

He had no more knives left to throw. There was nothing to do but run. He plunged into the forest where it was thickest, where he knew horses would have to slow to a walk. He scrambled up gullies, forded streams, and found at last the safety of a cave, one of the secret hideaways known only to his father and himself.

He lay back against the rock in the dark dank cave and tried to regain his breath and collect his thoughts. It was only now that he cried, for it was only now that he understood—that he was an orphan and quite alone in the world. Worse, he had run away and abandoned his own father.

A voice spoke to him from the mouth of the cave. "They did not kill him." It was a girl's voice. She stood silhouetted against the light: a willowy figure, a bow in her hand, a quiver of arrows on her back. "They did not kill him," she repeated. "We saw them. They took him away."

Filled with sudden hope, Robin started to his feet. "Are you sure?" He came toward her and then stopped dead.

"I am Marion." She was a young woman and not a girl at all. "And I wish you would not stare at me like that."

Her hair was white—not silver like an old person's, not fair as his mother's had been, but white, pure white. Her eyes seemed to glow red in the early-morning sun here. *But,* Robin thought, *there is no early-morning sun.*

"You're an Outcast, aren't you?" he whispered.

"We all are," said Marion quietly, and she turned and ran off.

Robin followed. As he emerged from the cold of the cave, he saw that the valley below him was filled with people, all of them gazing up at him and silent. Every one of them was dressed in the green of the forest. Some had long white hair to their shoulders, like the young woman's. Some looked like children at first, but they were not; they were dwarfs. There were hunchbacks among them; and it was one of these, the tallest, with a hunting horn in one hand, who stepped forward and spoke up.

"Your father was a good man. He fed the hungry. He fed the poor. We saw him. We watched him—we know everything and everyone that moves in the forest. We have to. Now he is captured, and you are one of us. Like us, you are an Outcast."

THREE

OUTCAST

The warning words of the village priest rang loud in Robin's head: "With a wolf, you walk away slowly, and he'll leave you alone. With a bear you look him in the eye and stay still. But pray you never ever see an Outcast. If you do, then run for your life. Outcasts are child-eaters. Outcasts are bloodsuckers." There was nowhere to run to, and no time either. Robin was soon surrounded by half a dozen Outcasts plucking at his sleeve and grinning up at him. There was a wildness in their eyes that alarmed him at first, but then he saw that they were smiling eyes. These were no cutthroats. These were no child-eaters. They were reaching up and touching his hair, his ears. But their touches were gentle, inquisitive.

One or two of them were babbling incoherently. Marion was there beside him.

"What are they saying?" Robin asked.

"They're just happy you're with us, can't you tell?"

"Can't they speak?"

"'Course they can, but not like you or me. The Sheriff caught them. He cut their tongues out—for the sport of it."

Then the hunchback who had first spoken to Robin was limping toward him. "I'm Will Scarlett," he said, holding out his hand. "You're welcome, Robin. Let's get you home."

And so Robin was led away into the forest by Will. They went at a run, but silently. Not a twig cracked; not a leaf rustled. All around him the forest flitted with darting shadows. The other Outcasts were coming too, all of them.

He looked everywhere for Marion but could not see her.

All day, it seemed, they traveled on—down deer tracks he'd never known, and deeper into the forest than he had ever been in his life. It was evening before they came to a cliff face that rose sheer out of the forest. It didn't stop the Outcasts. They plunged suddenly into the darkness of what seemed to be a vast cave. Then they were running along a tunnel toward a pinprick of light at the other end, out

across a clearing, down a ravine, and into thick forest again. When at long last they stopped, they stood still, breathing hard and listening.

Before Robin knew it, clamoring children were running toward him out of the trees. Many of these had Marion's white hair and pink eyes, and one hobbled along behind the others on a crutch, his leg twisted inward. There were lepers, too, Robin saw; their faces and fingers eaten away by the disease. He shied away, trying to fend them off, and was relieved to see Marion coming toward him. She took his hand and made off with him, shooing the children back.

They ate wild pig that night, all of them sitting in the shadows of a great crackling fire; but Robin had no stomach for it. It was not just that he felt their eyes watching him all the time, though that was part of it.

"You don't speak and you don't eat," said Will Scarlett. "What's the matter?"

"They'll hang him, won't they? My father, they'll hang him. You were there, weren't you? You saw it all. She said you did. Why didn't you help?"

"How?" said Will Scarlett. "With what? Would you have us fight with our bare hands against armed soldiers? You hurled your dagger and you ran. If you hadn't, then you'd be in Nottingham tonight, and tomorrow morning they'd be stretching your neck alongside your father's. How would that help? Tell me that. Your father's a good man, Robin, known everywhere in the forest for his kindness. And he's a wise man, too. He told you to run, didn't he? He knows what we know, that to survive is everything. We have to survive. Until good King Richard comes back from his crusade and brings us justice, we have to survive."

"So we wait, do we?" Robin protested. "We just wait until the King decides to come back. Meanwhile Guy of Gisbourne starves my mother to death and the Sheriff of Nottingham hangs my father. You wait if you like. I will not wait." He hurled his meat into the fire. "I will eat nothing until either my father is safe here in the forest, or I am dead."

Will Scarlett reached forward and gripped Robin by the wrist. "Do you think you are the only one to suffer at this butcher's hands? Look around you, Robin. A motley bunch of misfits, aren't we? There's every mutation you could imagine here. There's me, a hunchback, and there's half a dozen more the same. There're white-haired cagots, albinos—call them what you will—like Marion. There're simple folk who talk to the moon in puddles. There're lepers, there're one-legged beggars. Blind, deaf, dumb—we're all here, all misfits, all Outcasts. And why do you suppose we're here? Well, I'll tell you. Until the Sheriff came, most of us lived in Nottingham, as others live. Oh yes, people laughed at us, cursed us, threw their stones at us; but when you're like we are, you have to put up with that. Water off a duck's back.

"But the new Sheriff wanted us out. 'Human vermin,' he called us. 'The work of the devil.' And there were plenty of greedy priors and grasping abbesses to tell him he was right—if he paid them enough. To all of them, we were rats to be driven out. And he did it all legally, too. After all, it's the Sheriff who makes the laws, isn't it? He's the King's man in Nottingham. His word is the King's word and must be obeyed. First we weren't allowed to hold property in Nottingham . . . I was a tailor, and a good one. They closed me down . . . Then we weren't allowed to sleep within the city walls. We could work there by day, but every night they drove us out of the city and closed the gates. If you were caught inside after nightfall, you had your tongue pulled out.

"Winter nights were cold in the forest. A few risked it and hid in Nottingham. They lost their tongues for their pains. But he hadn't finished with us, oh no. He passed another law: All 'Outcasts'—he had a name for us now—were not to be allowed back in the city at all.

"So we left family, friends, everything and everyone, and we came here to live in the forest. The monks and priests put it about in the pulpits that we are devil-worshipers, child-eaters, bloodsuckers—I see you've heard the stories, too. So we live here and we survive. We have become creatures of the forest, creatures of the dark. And we wait for the King to come, to give us the justice we deserve. If we fight them in the open, then they will destroy us. They are too many and too strong.

"So we rob for what we need. The Sheriff's men look for us, but they cannot find us. We have lookouts all over Sherwood. If anyone comes into the forest, we know it. That's why we were there this morning." Will Scarlett held up Robin's father's great bow. "Here, your father dropped this. I found it. It's yours now, Robin."

Robin took his father's bow and held it in both hands. When he spoke, he spoke so softly, through his tears, that the Outcasts had to strain to listen. "I cannot sit here with you, warm by the fire, and think of my father alone and cold in his dungeon. My father cannot wait for the King's justice." He lifted his head. "I will not hide away like a rabbit all my life, bolting for my hole at the first sign of the Sheriff's men."

He saw the hurt come into Will Scarlett's eyes and at once wished he had not spoken so harshly. "I did not mean it like that," Robin went on. "You must do what you must do, and I must try to save my father. All I ask is that you lend me a dagger and some arrows, and set me on the road to Nottingham. I will do the rest myself."

Will Scarlett stood up and took Robin by the shoulders. "Any man would be proud to have a son like you," he said, and he gave Robin his dagger. "Here, have this. And you may have all the arrows you could want. Marion will take you to the road. God go with you, Robin."

Marion led the way up the ravine, across the clearing, through the black of the cave, and out into the forest beyond. She was light on her feet, and fast—so fast that she was often far in front of him. Robin would have lost sight of her entirely, were it not for her white hair moving through the trees ahead, like the moon dancing across water. Robin was beginning to wonder how much farther they would have to go when he saw her stop suddenly and crouch down in the undergrowth. He crouched beside her.

"Cross the stream ahead and follow the track," Marion whispered. "You'll be in Nottingham by dawn." Robin made as if to go, but she held him back. "Whatever happens," she said, "you will come back to the forest, won't you?"

Robin looked into her eyes and could scarcely bring himself to look away. He saw the fierce faith in them. She believed in him, believed in him utterly.

"I'll come back," he said. "And when I do, I'll bring Father with me." And he left her there without another word, and ran off into the night.

They were brave words but Robin felt far from brave. The thought of what he now had to do was daunting. He knew Nottingham. He had lived there as a little boy and been there often enough since, driving pigs or sheep to the market with his father. He had often gazed up at the great walls of the castle and seen the dungeons on the far side of the moat, white fingers gripping the bars over the windows. He had seen the cages in the marketplace, where the prisoners were brought to be mocked and abused all morning long before they were hanged at noon.

The Sheriff's men would be everywhere, lolling on street corners, roaming the streets in gangs, filling the taverns. There were hundreds of them, and they would be armed to the teeth.

Even now, as Robin came out of Sherwood into the light of morning and saw the walls of the city rising from the mist in the distance, he had no notion of how he would set about finding his father, still less how he would spirit him out of Nottingham.

Over the next rise, and he would see the gibbet by the bridge. Already he could see a few crows perched on a dead branch in a nearby oak tree, waiting. Here was where his father would be brought afterward, after they had hanged him in the market square.

Suddenly, a terrible thought came into Robin's mind. Perhaps they had already executed him. Usually they did it at midday, when the market square was crowded. They would haul the prisoner out of the cage and drag him screaming across the square, hang him, leave him there for an hour or two, and then bring him down to the gibbet. But maybe they had done it yesterday. Maybe they had taken Father back to Nottingham and hanged him at once. Why else would the crows be here now?

"No!" Robin cried aloud. "No!" And he ran down the hill, his legs pounding, head back, tears streaming down his face, praying and praying he was not too late. The mist lay thick along the riverbanks. There was no river to see, no bridge, and no gibbet. He could barely see the road in front of him now.

A horse loomed suddenly out of the mist. Robin was going so fast he had no hope of stopping. He careered into the animal at full speed. The horse reared up, throwing his rider out of the saddle.

As the mist lifted, the horse was cropping the grass busily beside the gibbet. Two men lay stretched out and senseless on the road.

Robin woke, his head throbbing, and sat up. Above him he saw the gibbet, stark against the morning sky, and below it a soldier, still unconscious. He looked to Robin like one of the Sheriff's men.

"Maybe you were heaven sent," Robin breathed. "My size, and a sword and a horse, too. All I could want."

He left the soldier trussed up and gagged under the bridge, and he emerged dressed in the mail and helmet of a Sheriff's man, a sword at his side, his father's bow over his shoulder. The horse was still eating, and easy enough to catch.

The gates of Nottingham were open when Robin got there; and from all around, people were streaming in for the market. Carried along by a crush of cattle and sheep and pigs and people, Robin rode up the narrow streets and into the market square. As expected, there were Sheriff's men loitering by the castle gates, and the market traders were setting out their stalls around the square. The scaffold stood in the center of it, the hanging rope swinging in the breeze. He had hoped to find his father already in one of the cages—it would have helped—but they were all empty. Robin was sitting on his horse, looking into the last of them, when a voice spoke up from behind him. "They tell me there's only one this morning for the rope. Killed the King's deer, he did. Not likely to be killing any more, is he? Poor beggar. Still, be a nice day for a hanging. I never miss one, you know. Never." The man squinted up at Robin, shielding his eyes against the white glare of the sun.

Robin left him and rode over the drawbridge into the castle courtyard. He did not think twice about what he was doing. In fact, he did not think about it at all. He just did it.

The courtyard was full of soldiers, and a blacksmith was shoeing from a smoky shed nearby. Robin tied up his horse and strode into the castle. He tried to look as if he knew where he was, all the time searching for a stairway that might lead him down to the dungeons below. No one challenged him. No one even appeared to notice he was there.

He saw two soldiers emerging from a narrow doorway below the main staircase. As he passed, one of them spoke. "Like Samson. Sheriff's own words."

"Sheriff's idea, was it, then?"

"I heard it was Guy of Gisbourne's," said the other. "He said that if this fellow was big like Samson, well then, maybe we'd better treat him like Samson. He did it himself, by all accounts." Robin's heart chilled. The stone stairs spiraled down into the darkness, lit only sparingly by torchlight. He came to a long corridor, two guards at the end of it sitting at a table playing dice. Robin walked toward them, hand on the hilt of his sword.

"You come for Samson?" said one of the guards. And he didn't even wait for a reply. He threw Robin the key. "In there," he said, pointing Robin to one of the dungeon doors. "Help yourself. He'll hang well, that one. Good and heavy." And they went back to the dice.

Robin unlocked the door and went in. His father sat on the stone floor, his head in his hands. When he looked up, Robin saw there was a bandage around his eyes and a rope around his neck. Robin crouched down beside him and helped him gently to his feet. "It's me, Father," he whispered. "It's Robin."

His father reached out, felt for Robin's face, and held it tight between his hands. "They've put out my eyes, Robin," he said. "I'm no use to you anymore, no use to anyone. Let me die, Robin. Just leave me and let me die."

FOUR

A BLOW
FOR FREEDOM

For some moments father and son clung together and wept silently.

"Until now, Father," said Robin, his voice hushed, "I have obeyed you in everything; but whether you're blind or not, I shall not leave you here to die." And he loosened the rope around his father's neck as he spoke. "We shall walk out of here, me as a Sheriff's man and you at the end of this rope as my prisoner. Just play the games I play, Father, and we shall both live."

"What for? What is there to live for?"

"To fight. We will fight this tyrant, and we shall bring him to his knees, I promise you—if it takes my whole lifetime." He pulled gently on the rope. "Forgive me, Father, but from now on I must treat you as they would. It won't be for long. And curse me back as much as you like, it'll be all the better if you do." He took a deep breath and then shouted into his father's face. "Up, you scumbag! Up!" He threw open the door and dragged his father out past the guards.

"A bit early, aren't you?" said one of them.

"Sir Guy of Gisbourne's orders," Robin said. "Come on, Samson, move yourself, you great oaf." And Robin jerked on the rope and hauled his father up the winding stairs, across the great hall of the castle, and out into the courtyard beyond. Through the arched gateway Robin could see the milling crowd in the market square—and the horse waiting, tied to one of the cages, where he had left it. There was still the wide courtyard to cross, and then the drawbridge, and at the far end of it were the castle guards. Somehow Robin and his father had to get past them without arousing suspicion. Slipping past unnoticed would be impossible. Robin went around behind his father, drew his sword, and jabbed him in the back, none too gently.

"When I kick you, Father," he whispered, "fall over. Understand?"

His father staggered forward across the courtyard, through the gateway, and out onto the drawbridge, arms outstretched in front of him. Robin was taunting him and prodding him on, much to the delight of all the onlookers.

"I'll show you, Samson. Kill the King's deer, would you!" Once on the

drawbridge and close to the guards, he stepped back and took a running kick at his father, who stumbled to his knees, groping in front of him, cursing and crying at the same time. Robin laid into him with the flat of his sword and kicked him again. "Up, you beggar. Get up." Then he called out to the guards. "Here, give us a hand, will you? Sir Guy wants him paraded around the square before we put him in his cage. We'll stick him up on that horse. They'll see him better."

So, between them, the guards heaved him up onto the horse. "Once around the square and into his cage," said Robin, taking the reins over the horse's head to lead it. "That's what Sir Guy said, so that's what I'll do. It'll be the last time this one'll be going to market." The guards laughed at that and watched them go.

Robin walked away as slowly as he dared, calling out as he went. "Look at this! Look at this! See what happens to poachers. We put his eyes out and we're hanging him at noon. Death to all poachers! . . . Throw what you like at him. Just don't hit me, that's all." And the crowd howled with laughter and began to throw anything they could, rotten apples, turnips, even pig's muck. Much of it missed, but enough found its target to encourage others to do the same.

They were halfway around the market square now, at the point farthest from the Sheriff's men, who were still lounging by the bridge. Feigning to adjust the girth, Robin leaped nimbly up behind his father, put his heels to the horse's side, and rode off past the traders, through the crowd—who seemed to see it as part of the fun, particularly when he caught a rotten apple and squeezed it over his father's head.

Robin gave only one glance backward as he turned out of the square and down the street. The Sheriff's men were just beginning to notice his flight; one of them was running after him and shouting for him to stop. They would be after him soon enough now. Robin just hoped and prayed he had enough of a head start.

"Hold on, Father!" he cried. "Just hold on." Scattering people and pigs and sheep in all directions, he thundered down the streets, through the city gate, and out into the open country beyond.

The guards at the gate could only gape. He was past them and gone before anyone could even try to stop him.

But now came the real test. There were four or five miles of open farmland before they could reach the safety of Sherwood. A look over his shoulder, and Robin saw the chase was on. The Sheriff's men were through the city gates and already closer behind than he had thought possible; twenty of them, maybe more, and every time he looked they were gaining on them.

The horse labored under the combined weight of Robin and his father, his head nodding lower and lower as Robin drove his legs on. Sherwood lay up ahead—just the hill to climb; but it was a long hill and the horse could barely make a trot by now. Desperately Robin looked around for somewhere to hide, anywhere. But there was nothing but hedgerows and haystacks between them and the forest. They had to keep going.

He could hear the pounding of the hooves behind him now. And then the first arrow flew by, missing them; but he knew the men were well in range. He pushed his father forward to lie over the horse's neck and then lay on top of him.

"We'll make it!" he cried, but it was more in hope than in belief. The horse's legs and flanks were white with lather; he had given his all, and Robin knew it.

Robin looked up. The road narrowed ahead as it entered the forest. Just a minute more, maybe two. But all the while the horse was slowing, weaving. At this rate, even if they reached the forest ahead of the Sheriff's men, even if they were not hit by a lucky arrow, the Sheriff's men would be so close behind that there would be no escape, even in Sherwood. The horse was staggering, his lungs wheezing. Any farther and he would die under them. Still short of the forest, Robin dismounted quickly, helped his father down, and then hand in hand they ran for the trees. More arrows flew past them, some far too close for comfort. Robin wanted to dodge and swerve as his father had taught him, but with his father stumbling beside him, he could not. Speed was all that would save them.

Then they were in under the trees and swallowed by shade. For just a few brief moments, Robin knew they would be invisible to the Sheriff's men as the soldiers followed out of the sunlight and into the dark of the forest. Hauling his father

behind him, Robin plunged into the undergrowth and then went to ground in a thicket, lying still, as fawns do. There were voices in the forest now, barked commands, the jingle of harnesses, horses breathing hard, pawing the ground. Robin looked up into the trees above him.

Something caught his eye, a white moon in the branches that suddenly fell out and downward. A great whooping filled the forest and the Sheriff's men cried out, but their screams were cut suddenly short.

By the time Robin stood up moments later, the slaughter was over. The bodies of the Sheriff's men lay where they had been struck down. Their terrified horses could still be heard galloping away into the forest. And from out of the trees all around him came the Outcasts, Will Scarlett among them.

"We wouldn't have been here but for Marion," Will said, looking around in horror at the dead.

"Where is she?" Robin asked.

"Behind you, Robin," said Will, and when Robin turned he saw she was leading his father toward him.

Robin took his father's hands in his. "I'm here, Father, I'm here."

"Who are these people?" his father asked.

"Outcasts," Robin said. "But they are my friends, Father; and your friends, too, I think. And if they will have us, Father, then we shall live with them in Sherwood. Together we shall become strong, strong enough to put the fear of God into the Sheriff and Sir Guy of Gisbourne. For what the Sheriff has done to you, Father, to

Mother, and to these good people, he must be punished. And I will not wait for King Richard to do it. Today we struck a blow for freedom, but only the first blow."

There was a commotion, and through the crowd of Outcasts came one of the Sheriff's men, his head bloodied, his eyes darting with terror. He was being dragged along by two triumphant Outcasts. "Shall we cut his throat for him, Will?" said one of them.

Will Scarlett looked long at Robin before he spoke, and then Will handed him his hunting horn. "Ask Robin," he said. "I think Robin speaks for us all now. If we are to fight this monster, and when I look on Robin's father it seems we must, then I am not the man to lead you. I am a man of peace. I am too old, too tired. Robin may be young, he may not yet have a wise head on his shoulders; but after what he has done today, we cannot doubt his courage. I say he is the man we need if we are to bring down this butcher of Nottingham. Robin speaks for me."

"And for me," said Marion quietly.

"And me! And me!" came the clamoring chorus from all around them.

Then, as he looked at Marion, Robin knew that it was not only faith and trust he saw in her eyes, it was the glow of love; and he knew, too, that it was a reflected glow. The love that surged between them, although unspoken, gave him heart. With Marion beside him he could do anything, be anyone. No more a boy, no more a mere son, in that moment as he gazed at her he grew into himself. He needed only his father's blessing.

"What do you say, Father?" Robin asked.

27

"I say you saved my life, Robin. I say you speak for me—and by the sounds of it you speak for us all—but only so long as we all want you to. The other way lies tyranny. Be warned of that, my son."

Robin turned then to the Sheriff's man. "We shall not kill you, friend," he began. "But tell the Sheriff from me, tell Sir Guy of Gisbourne—tell everyone in Nottingham—that the Outcasts rule here in Sherwood, that we rule in the King's name. We will eat what we can kill, the King's deer and the King's salmon, for we are the King's subjects and we need to eat. Tell him this, too: that if he or his lackeys or anyone else comes through Sherwood, then he pays taxes to us. Tell him that, unlike him, we shall take only what a man can afford to pay. Tell him that with the taxes we take, we shall feed the hungry and clothe the poor. And tell the Sheriff this, too: that when our good King Richard returns from the holy wars, he shall know of the Sheriff's tyranny, for I shall tell him myself face-to-face. Go now."

The Sheriff's man backed away but did not turn to run. "Who are you?" he breathed.

"I am Robin of Sherwood, Robin Hood, son of Martin, whose eyes the Sheriff has blinded forever. Now go—and go quickly, before I change my mind."

The man turned and stumbled out of the forest, looking again and again over his shoulder, expecting an arrow in his back at any moment and unable to believe his luck.

"Well, Robin," said Will Scarlett, putting an arm around Robin's shoulder, "you have well and truly set the cat among the pigeons, haven't you?"

"But we are not pigeons anymore, Will," said Robin. "We are hawks, and like hawks we will come at them out of the sun, strike hard, and soar away out of sight. But first we have to sharpen our talons, for they will be back, and back with a vengeance too. We must be ready for them."

Never had the King's venison tasted as sweet as it did that night. To the Outcasts every mouthful only served to feed their newfound defiance. The tale of the battle was told and told again and again, until they had killed a hundred of the Sheriff's men and not a mere twenty. If they made Robin tell them once how he had rescued his father, then they made him tell them a dozen times, and each time the laughter rang louder through the trees.

Marion, though, was not there to hear it. Among the Outcasts, it was only she who had healing powers, so she took Robin's father aside and bathed his eyes and dressed them. Then she sat with him until he slept. Only then did she leave him and seek out Robin.

She found him sitting alone, away from the fire, his back against a tree, his father's bow at his side. He held out a hand to her, and she sat down beside him.

"He is sleeping," she said. "The pain must be terrible, but he never speaks of it. He speaks only of you."

Robin looked at her. "Without you, I do not think I can do this thing," he said.

"Then you can do it, Robin," she replied, brushing his hair from his eyes and then holding his face in her hands. "For you will never be without me. I will be with you always, just so long as you never change, Robin. Be always as you are now."

"I will try," Robin replied, kissing the palm of her hand. "I will try."

FIVE

DEAD OR ALIVE

 It was just as Will Scarlett had always feared. For years the Outcasts had cowered deep in Sherwood Forest, known of and feared, too, as sprites and spriggans and devils were feared. But they had always kept themselves to themselves, and for the most part they had been left in peace. They had been a threat to no one.

Now all that had changed. The story of how Robin Hood had snatched away his blind father from right under the Sheriff's nose, and of how the Outcasts had ambushed the Sheriff's men in Sherwood and left all but one of them dead, had spread like wildfire through the city of Nottingham and out into every village and hamlet for miles around. For most of those who heard it, it was a tale to be told again and again, and reveled in, for it gave some glimmer of hope for freedom from the hated tyrant. But for the Sheriff himself; for Sir Guy of Gisbourne, his lieutenant and companion in cruelty; for the lords and ladies, priors and abbesses who had all grown rich and fat on the Sheriff's plunder of the poor, this was an outrage, a rebellion that had to be put down savagely, before the flames of it engulfed them and destroyed them all.

For weeks and months afterward, the Sheriff sent Sir Guy of Gisbourne and his soldiers searching through the forest; but the soldiers, too, had heard the stories of Robin and the Outcasts, an invisible, silent enemy that fell on you from the trees above so you never even saw the one who cut your throat. Neither the soldiers nor Sir Guy of Gisbourne himself had much stomach for such a fight, so they kept close to the tracks and never dared to venture far into the forest. Every patrol returned empty-handed and the Sheriff of Nottingham fumed in his castle, for he knew the people were laughing at him secretly. And no tyrant can ever bear to be laughed at.

But worse was still to come for him. Travelers on their way north from London had to pass through Sherwood; there was no other road. They would arrive almost daily in Nottingham with terrifying stories of how they had been robbed in

Sherwood Forest, how they had been stopped and forced to surrender all they had—jewels, money, even their clothes sometimes. They spoke of a young man dressed, as the robbers all were, in Lincoln green. There was a girl with him too, a cagot with hair as white as snow. There were dozens of them—some said hundreds—a small army of dwarfs and jibberers and more albino cagots; men, women, and children with hunchbacks and harelips; and lepers, too. And this young man—their leader, he seemed to be—was always very polite. He introduced himself as Robin Hood and often asked to be remembered to the Sheriff of Nottingham and Sir Guy of Gisbourne. He would tell them, as he sent them on their way, that if they were good Christian folk then they should be happy to give away all they had, for everything they gave would go to the poor and needy. He called it "The Sherwood Tax." It was the Outcasts who ruled in Sherwood now, he said, so in the future all taxes were to be paid to them and not to the Sheriff. Some travelers he even invited to eat with the Outcasts around the fire. The toast at the end of the meal was always the same: "To the return of good King Richard!"

Infuriated by every such report, and vowing he would not rest until he had the head of Robin Hood, the Sheriff sent to London, to his friend Prince John, for help. With King Richard, John's elder brother, away on a crusade to capture the holy city of Jerusalem from the Saracens, and unlikely to return for some time, if ever, the Prince was effectively king in his place. A callous, greedy, and scheming man, he had only one idea in his head: to usurp his brother's throne while he was away, and by any means.

Chief among John's fellow conspirators was the Sheriff of Nottingham, so when the call came for help to put down a band of rebels who were openly loyal to King Richard, Prince John not only agreed at once but came himself, at the head of five hundred soldiers. So that the people would know once and for all who ruled in Sherwood, and in England, too, the Prince and the Sheriff joined forces and rode together through Sherwood, a thousand men or more.

The Outcasts lay low and watched unseen from the trees.

But the Sheriff had something else in mind, too. He sent the soldiers far and wide to burn out the homes of suspected sympathizers—yeomen, foresters, farmers, charcoal-burners, anyone. A few resisted and were hanged in the market square below Nottingham Castle, "to teach everyone a lesson they won't ever forget," as the Sheriff put it. And as they still hung there that evening, Prince John proclaimed from the castle walls that the man called Robin Hood was condemned

as an outlaw, as were all Outcasts. They were to be hunted down like the animals they were, and a hundred pounds would be paid for Robin Hood, dead or alive.

When word of the price on Robin's head reached the Outcasts' encampment deep in Sherwood, Robin merely laughed it off. But no one else did, least of all Marion.

Will Scarlett was fearful, too, and said so. "We must be careful, Robin. We have stirred up a hornets' nest and made them mad. Why don't we just hide ourselves away again, like we used to? Let them forget about us. Let's make them think we're not here, that they've won. Why not let everyone pass freely through the forest, for a while at least?"

And Robin's father spoke up, too. "Will is right, Robin. We can still feed the hungry. We can still help the poor. We'll just do it by night, secretly, that's all—like I used to, remember?"

Robin listened to them both and saw at once the wisdom in what they said, but there were others among the Outcasts urging him to attack the castle, and now, while Prince John was still there.

"Kill two birds with one stone!"

"Three. Don't forget Guy of Gisbourne."

"The people will rise up with us, Robin. Strike now!"

"We should string them up, the three of them, side by side, like common criminals."

"And give the crows a good feasting!"

All evening the Outcasts argued back and forth, and Robin listened until he could stand it no more. He went off by himself to his tree, as he often did when he needed to think things out on his own. He knew the band would all do just what he decided, out of love, out of loyalty, and without question. But the responsibility of it lay heavily on his young shoulders. As he sat there under his tree, his head told him that Will was right, that his father was right; but in his heart he longed to seek out the Sheriff and Prince John and Sir Guy of Gisbourne and punish them for their cruel reprisals. Marion came to find him as the last of the evening sun left the sky.

"They are right, all of them are right," she said, knowing his thoughts well, as she always did. "That's what makes it so difficult. So maybe we should do everything they say."

"What do you mean?"

"Maybe we should hide ourselves away, as Will says, lie low. But we shouldn't just hide. You said it once yourself. We should make ourselves strong. We are only fifty—seventy with the children. No one can hide better than we can. We know every inch of the forest; but as we are, we are no match for the Sheriff's men in open combat. We can ambush, yes, strike quickly and fade away into the forest again. But to do more than that, and we will have to, we need to learn how to shoot straight, how to handle a sword. And we need more fighters alongside us, too, the best we can find. We need weapons, more weapons, better weapons. Then we can attack the wolf in his lair. But we have to wait until we are ready. When the time comes to strike, Robin, you will know it."

Robin drew her down beside him. "But will the time ever come, Marion?"

"If God wills it," she replied. "And He will, if we have faith, if we are true to Him and do His work. After all, He brought us to safety in the forest, didn't He? And He brought us together, didn't He?"

"Yes," said Robin, reaching out to touch her hair. ". . . So white. So white."

She caught his hand and held it against her cheek. "Do you wish my hair were black, raven black? Are you thinking I have the eyes of a ferret?"

"I was just thinking that I love you."

"I know you were." Marion laughed. "I just wanted to hear you say it."

So for the next few years Robin and the Outcasts hid themselves away in deepest Sherwood; and sure enough, as Will Scarlett had hoped, the Sheriff came to believe his problems in Sherwood Forest were over. He trumpeted it about in Nottingham and at the court of Prince John that Robin Hood must be dead; and that even if he wasn't, then he was too frightened of the Sheriff of Nottingham to dare show his face again.

But Sir Guy of Gisbourne knew better, for he had his spies everywhere, and they told him how in the markets and taverns, and around the fires at night, people still talked of Robin Hood and his Outcasts in the forest. All the while, the poor were being fed—somehow. Burned-down houses were rebuilt, stolen animals replaced—somehow.

Sir Guy of Gisbourne had little doubt that Robin Hood was still perfectly alive, and kicking, too. He told the Sheriff so, time and time again; but the Sheriff brushed him aside haughtily, preferring to hear only what he wanted to believe.

"Don't you worry yourself, Guy," he would crow. "Robin Hood is down among the worms. We've seen the last of him, I tell you—unless, of course, you believe in ghosts."

All this while neither Robin nor the Outcasts had wasted any time. His father,

blind though he was, had taken it upon himself to tutor every one of them in the longbow. There was not one now who could not fashion a bow from the yew, and arrows from the ash. And they could use them, too. Boy or girl, young or old, Robin's father made them all practice every day, so that by now every single Outcast who could hold a bow could shoot straight and true, some of them almost as well as Robin himself.

With Will Scarlett for his eyes, Robin's father was never happier than when he was teaching some young Outcast how to judge the arc of flight, how to let fly without jerking. Left alone for too long, he was inclined to moods of dark despair, so the Outcasts saw to it that he always had someone with him. All of them had known despair at one time or another, so they knew instinctively when they were needed.

He particularly treasured the time when Marion would sit by him and tell him the stories her family had brought with them from France a hundred years before: stories of great mountains that touched the sky, of bears and wolves. He could listen to her stories forever; he could never hear enough of them. He knew, without seeing, what everyone else knew, that Robin and Marion had become inseparable.

Marion spoke of it one day when Robin was out hunting. "It's not just me that loves him," she said, "we all do."

"Maybe, but I love him as a father loves his son, and you love him as a woman loves a man. For the rest, they worship him and I wish they would not. Worship is for God, not man. I fear it will be too much for him. Stay close to him, Marion. He will need you, as a man needs his eyes."

Each year there were fewer stags to be found in the forest, so Robin and the Outcasts had to travel farther and farther from home in their search for meat. Hinds there were, and in plenty, but Robin had forbidden all killing of hinds unless they were old or wounded.

It was June and the trees were in full leaf, and the deer difficult to spot in the dappled shadows of the forest. The Outcasts had gone for days without a kill. They were all weary of it and wanted to go home. Robin wanted to be on his own for a while, to collect his thoughts. More and more he found that he could be himself only with Marion, that he was tired of playing the leader, of smiling when he did not wish to.

"We'll split up, twos and threes, south, north, east, and west. Maybe we'll be lucky . . . But be careful. We're close to the edge of the forest here, so keep an eye out for the Sheriff's men. You never know. Be back by sunset and I'll meet you down by the river, over there." And off they went.

Robin had it in mind to hide down by the river and wait for a stag to come down to drink. But he was about to break both of his own golden rules: No one was ever to sleep unless guarded; and no one was ever to be separated from their horn or their weapon. Quite forgetting all this, Robin squatted down under the shade of a great alder tree overhanging the river and waited. Kingfishers flitted up and down the river, flashes of fire in the sunlight. A heron landed nearby and waded on his stick legs into the shallows to fish. No stag came, but there were footprints enough to keep Robin hopeful.

After a while, though, he became thirsty. He left his bow, his arrows, and his horn under the tree and went down to the river to drink, cupping his hands in the water. The water was so cold and so inviting, he didn't think twice. He took off his jerkin and jumped in. It was not that far to the other side, and the current seemed gentle enough. So he swam across and stretched out on the bank in the warmth of the sun to get his breath back.

He had closed his eyes against the glare of the sunlight and was drifting off into a welcome sleep when he felt a cold shadow come over him. He looked up into a round, red, grinning face; and there was a sword at his throat.

SIX

TUCK AND MUCH AND LITTLE JOHN

 "I'm looking for Robin Hood. Do you know the rogue?"

Robin saw the man was wearing the brown habit of a friar.

"I've heard of him," Robin replied. "Now, will you let me up?"

But the friar put his foot on Robin's chest and would not let him move.

"Tell me where I can find him and I might let you live, by God's good grace," said the friar, pressing the point of his sword into Robin's neck just enough to draw blood.

"Cross the river and just keep going," said Robin. "You won't find him. He'll find you. And when he does, friend, you'd better watch out. He doesn't much like friars, especially the rich, fat ones."

The friar laughed and twisted the blade of his sword. "Does he not, indeed? Well, now, that's mighty unfortunate, because as you see I'm very fat; and I'm very rich, too, as it happens, by God's good grace. In my sack here I have all the silver and gold I could steal. I suppose I'm about the richest, fattest friar you'll ever be likely to meet. And do you know something else, young man? I've this terrible aversion to water. I can't abide wet feet. So how, I ask myself, how am I going to cross this river?" He hit his head with the palm of his hand. "Of course. Of course. Silly me. You can take me, can't you? You can carry me, me and my sack of treasures. You won't mind, will you?"

The sword at Robin's throat left him little choice. Besides, he had it already in mind that if he could get himself back across to the other side of the river, then at least he would have his sword close at hand, and his horn to call for help if need be—though by the shape of the friar, Robin did not imagine for one moment that he would need any help.

So, standing in the shadows with the river tugging at his ankles, he braced himself and waited for the fat friar to jump on his back. When he did, it was all Robin could do to stand upright. The friar must have weighed as much as a full-

39

grown stag. Robin stumbled out into the river, the friar spurring him on like a donkey and whacking him with the flat of his sword.

"Giddyap! Giddyap, you skinny nag!" he cried. And Robin ground his teeth in fury and staggered on. Twice he fell to his knees in the water, and the friar cursed him, whacked him again, and drove him on. When at last Robin reached the bank and sank down exhausted, the friar stood back, leaned on his sword, and laughed till the tears ran down his face, the whole fat bulk of him wobbling like jelly. Robin saw his moment had come. His sword stood where he had left it, against the alder tree. He sprang to his feet, grabbed it, and with one swipe knocked the friar's sword from his grasp. Suddenly the friar was not laughing anymore.

"Now, fat man!" cried Robin, his sword deep into the friar's several chins. "You shall carry me back over the river—not once, but twice; there and back, because I am only half your weight. Only fair, I think. Then we'll be even, and you can go your way, and I'll go mine. No hard feelings, eh?"

"By God's good grace," said the friar, "you're a fine and fair man, even if you are a mite skinny. Hop on; I won't even feel you're there."

Sure enough, the friar strode out across the river so fast that Robin barely had any time to enjoy his triumph before he found himself being carried back again.

They were halfway back when the friar suddenly stopped. "Get on, you great donkey, get on," Robin bellowed in his ear, kicking him on.

But the friar was lifting his nose and sniffing the air. "By God's good grace," he said, "you stink like an old badger. What you need is a good bath." And with that he leaned forward and tossed Robin off his back.

Robin was not easily roused to anger, but as he sat there soaking and cold in the river, listening to the fat friar's mocking laughter, his temper suddenly snapped. He charged out of the river, snatched up his sword, and went for the friar like a wild thing.

"Temper, temper," scoffed the friar, standing his ground and parrying every frantic thrust and slash with consummate ease. Worst of all, though, the friar would not stop laughing.

The man was playing with him, and Robin knew it. This only served to infuriate him all the more. He was losing and there was nothing he could do about it. As his father had told him often enough: Once you think you might lose, then you will lose. Before he knew it, Robin saw his sword flying through the air and felt again the friar's sword at his throat.

"By God's good grace, you're an angry young man with a wicked temper. All I asked, and politely it was, too, was where I might find this Robin Hood."

"Well, look no further, friar," Robin said, pushing aside the sword. "You're looking at him."

"You? Robin Hood? But I heard he outwitted the Sheriff, Sir Guy of Gisbourne, and the whole miserable bunch of them all by himself. I heard he could handle a sword better than any man alive."

"I'm better with a bow and arrow," Robin replied sheepishly.

The friar lowered his sword. "You really are Robin Hood, leader of the Outcasts? But you're little more than a boy."

Robin retrieved his horn from under the tree and blew on it three times, long and hard, the Outcasts' call for help. "You'll see soon enough," said Robin, feretting in the friar's sack. He drew out a golden cross. "So you robbed a church, did you?"

"In a manner of speaking, yes," replied the friar, who was suddenly serious now. "And I'll tell you why. I was staying at Fountains Abbey, with the monks, as I often do when I pass by. And one Sunday morning from the pulpit, I spoke up for Robin Hood and his Outcasts, for all they were doing for the poor, for the unloved, for those our dear Lord loves more than anyone. The Sheriff heard of it, drove the monks out, and took their abbey from them. He gave it over to that she-devil the Abbess of Kirkleigh, sister to the Sheriff, and Guy of Gisbourne's lover too—did you know that? I may be a sinner. I drink too much, I know it, and my midriff vouches for my indulgence in at least one of the seven deadly sins, but compared to that witch I am an angel—an angel, I tell you! So I went back and rescued what I could of the abbey's treasures before she got her evil hands on them. It is little enough, but it belongs to God, and God would want it spent where it is most needed. So I came to look for Robin Hood, to help him help the poor, and to lend him my prayers and my sword, if he wants them."

"Oh, he wants them, good friar," said Robin, and even as he spoke the Outcasts came running out of the trees all around; it was all Robin could do to prevent them throwing themselves at the friar.

"Leave him be!" he cried. "He is an enemy of our enemy, so he's our friend. Besides which, he'd cut you all into little pieces with that sword of his—believe me. And look what he has brought us." Robin held up the sack and shook it at them. "Gold and silver. Treasure to feed hungry mouths, lots of them. This friar, unlike most, is a true friar and worthy of his calling, a Christian man. Welcome to our band, friar."

And when they embraced, the friar squeezed him so hard that Robin felt his ribs might crack. "Do you have a name, friar?" he said.

"Brother Ignatius. But that's a terrible mouthful, so my friends call me Tuck, Friar Tuck."

So Friar Tuck came to live among them in Sherwood. He ate enough for three good men, but to the Outcasts he was worth every mouthful. He was not a fellow to be argued with, and they soon knew it. He set up a candlelit chapel in the cave beyond the clearing and made it plain that he expected everyone to be there each Sunday when he rang the bell for mass. Very few dared or wanted to stay away.

Sundays he kept for the healing of the soul. "We're arming ourselves for Christ," he would say. But every other day he spent schooling the Outcasts in the art of swordsmanship, so that the forest rang now to the clash of steel on steel and Friar Tuck's infectious laughter. Loud buffoon, fierce warrior, wise priest, Tuck was a man of many parts, and it was he as much as anyone who bound the band of Outcasts together and made a fighting force of them. Each one was now highly skilled with sword and bow, but although a few outsiders had trickled in to join them in Sherwood, there were still not enough of them to attack the Sheriff and Sir Guy of Gisbourne in their strongholds.

Tuck did not mince his words; he never did. "We can't just wait here, Robin, until folk decide to join us. We have to go out and recruit them—that's what the Lord Jesus did, by God's good grace. And we need more weapons, better weapons, swords, spears, shields. Either we go out and steal them—and we can't do that without waking the Sheriff up—or we make them. We need a blacksmith. And there's another thing. You're all of you a deal too small and skinny, if you don't mind my saying so. I could blow most of you over with one snotty sneeze. We have to be able to fight them with our bare hands if necessary. You've got to be strong. You've got to learn how to wrestle." And he patted his great stomach as he went on. "And don't look at me. I can't teach you, not with this belly of mine. And Robin can't either. He's all whippet and no hound. We need to find someone who can teach us how we can snap Sir Guy of Gisbourne's miserable neck with a tweak of the wrist, or squeeze the life out of the Sheriff of Nottingham. A little faith, Robin, and by God's good grace, we'll find the men we need."

They were to find the wrestler first.

Much was a miller's son. All his life he had worked with his father, carrying sacks of wheat from the granary to the mill, and then sacks of flour from the mill to the cart outside. They worked every waking hour God gave them and they sold their flour to anyone who would buy it.

The Sheriff of Nottingham bought all the flour he needed from Much's father, but he always grumbled that the prices were too high. Much's father, unlike many other millers, was no cheat. He always gave fair measures for a fair price, and so he refused to lower the price even when the Sheriff threatened to burn down his mill. Unfortunately, when it came to threats, the Sheriff was always as good as his word. This time he did not send his men to do his dirty work, as he so often did; he meted out the punishment himself—he enjoyed that kind of thing from time to time, particularly if there was little or no danger.

It was dawn, and Much was out rabbit-trapping when the Sheriff came with his men. Much's father was already at his milling. The Sheriff's men shut the door of the mill and barred it. Then they tossed burning branches in through the windows and set it on fire.

If there was one single thing that alarmed the Outcasts, it was fire. They all knew, as every forester does, just how fast a wind-fanned fire can race through the treetops, faster than a man can run. A lookout saw the smoke rising from the edge of the forest and sounded his horn. By the time Robin and the Outcasts reached

the mill, it had burned to the ground. They found Much, the miller's son, sitting and staring into the ashes, his face blackened with smoke and smeared with tears. He looked up at Robin.

"I should have been here. I was too late. They burned him. They burned my father alive."

"The Sheriff?" Robin asked.

"I saw him riding off," said Much. "He was laughing. They were all laughing."

Friar Tuck took him by the arms and helped him to his feet. Much was a massive man. He towered above Tuck and was just about as broad as he was high.

"By God's good grace, I know you," said Tuck. "You're the wrestler I saw at Nottingham Fair, aren't you? Didn't you throw ten men inside as many minutes? I'd know you anywhere. I was one of the ten!" He turned to Robin. "Didn't I tell you, Robin? Didn't I say to have faith?"

"Then heaven be praised," said Robin, "for you're just the man we're looking for, Much. Teach us to fight as well as you, and we'll build up your mill better than it ever was. What d'you say?"

Much, the miller's son, looked down at Robin and wiped away the last of his tears. "You're Robin Hood, aren't you?" And he laid his great hands on Robin's shoulders. "You can leave the mill as it is. I have milled my last sack of flour. If I can be of service, if I can put my strength to some good use, then all I ask in return is food in my belly, a warm place to lay my head, and the chance when the time comes to hang the cursed Sheriff of Nottingham for what he did to my father. Is it a bargain?"

"A bargain," said Robin, "and a promise."

And from that moment on the two of them became the closest of friends, always comfortable in each other's company. Hugely different as they were in shape and size, they were about the same age. A quiet giant and never far from Robin's side, Much soon became known as "the shadow." They spoke little, nor did they need to, so closely did they seem to understand one another—perhaps because the Sheriff had wreaked much the same havoc in both their young lives.

Much proved to be a tireless, patient teacher. He taught the Outcasts everything he knew, so that within months all of them were fighting fit. They were ready. Now, every one of them, however twisted and bent, could defend himself or herself, and most were more than a match for any Sheriff's man. They were champing at the bit, straining to be let loose at the Sheriff, to do what they had been trained to do.

But Will Scarlett and Robin's father still counseled caution. The Outcasts had only a couple dozen rusty swords and a few spears between them, hardly enough to attack Nottingham Castle. All the blacksmiths they knew of were in the pay of the Sheriff and his armorer, and none of them could be trusted.

Robin, like most of them, began to despair of ever finding a smith. But not Tuck. "The Lord brought us Much, did he not?" he said. "Remember what He told us: 'Seek and ye shall find.' And so we shall, by God's good grace. We shall find ourselves a blacksmith."

To keep the Outcasts happy, Robin arranged endless wrestling matches and archery competitions—which he was careful not to win too often. There were mock battles, mock ambushes. The weeks passed, and the Outcasts searched the villages far and wide; but still they could not find the man they wanted.

Like everyone else, Robin yearned for action. Marion did what she could to persuade him to be patient. "Bide your time, Robin," she would tell him. "Why rush into danger? Let's just live while we can, and be happy. He'll turn up sooner or later, you'll see."

And she was right. They did find a blacksmith; or rather, he found them.

Robin was fishing for sea trout. It was the first run of the year, and they were rising everywhere, but difficult to catch. Much was with him, as he always was, and Friar Tuck as well. It was a warm summer's day and the storm flies were low over the water. Tuck was squatting down at the river's edge, busy gutting a sea trout for their lunch, when someone called out to them from across the river.

"A fine fish." The voice was as big as the man. "I shall have that for my lunch, I think."

"I don't think you will," replied Friar Tuck.

"Tell you what, friar," said the russet-bearded giant, walking toward the bridge. "You meet me on this bridge. And if I topple you into the river, then I can have your fish. How's that?"

Friar Tuck snorted with laughter. "By God's good grace, I'll do the toppling, my friend, not you." And he drew his sword.

"One arrow past his nose would send him packing," said Robin, reaching for his own bow.

"Waste of a good arrow. Just look at him," Tuck scoffed. "He's a beggar of a fellow, dressed in nothing but rags. He doesn't look as if he's eaten in a week. And he's carrying nothing but a staff. Don't you worry, Robin, I'll soon fix him."

Robin and Much looked on as the two men met on the bridge in the middle of the river.

"You strike first, friar," said the stranger.

And Friar Tuck swung up his great sword and struck. Again and again he struck, but the staff was always there blocking the blow. He whirled his sword high above his head, thinking to cut the staff in two. The next moment his sword was sent flying into the water and he found himself defenseless. The stranger smiled and then thrust the end of his staff deep into Tuck's belly. Bent double, all the wind driven out of him, Tuck staggered toward the edge of the bridge, and the stranger's boot helped topple him over the side and into the river.

With a roar like a bear, Much charged on to the bridge. "To get our fish," he cried, "you'll have to pass me first."

"But you have no weapon," said the stranger.

"I need none," replied Much, and he lunged forward to grab the staff.

As Much came at him, the man stepped nimbly sideways and simply prodded him into the river.

At once Robin was on the bridge, an arrow strung to his bow and aimed at the man's heart. "Move just one step and I shall kill you."

The stranger sighed and shook his head sadly. "Is there no one in good King Richard's land who will give a poor fellow a meal?" he said. "Everywhere I go I tell them I fought alongside the King in the Holy Land, and what do they do but curse me and drive me out. Richard is dead, they say, and Prince John is king in his place. It's not true, I tell them. Richard is not dead. He is held prisoner in Austria, and why? Because his brother, John, will not pay the ransom for his release. They don't believe me. They think I'm mad and they beat me black and blue. I have had enough. So shoot on, fine fellow. Your arrow holds no fear for me."

Robin lowered his bow. "You've given my friends a good soaking." He laughed. "But anyone who is a friend of King Richard is our friend, too. Come across and we'll eat the fish together."

As the fish cooked slowly over the fire, the stranger could scarcely take his eyes from it. When it was ready, he ate it head to tail, stripping every morsel of pink flesh from the bone. The others looked on, mouths watering. "I hope it chokes you," said Friar Tuck, still smarting from his dunking in the river.

The stranger reached over and picked up Tuck's sword.

"A fine weapon," he said, running his thumb along the blade, "but blunt."

"What do you know of weapons?" said Friar Tuck, snatching back his sword.

"I told you. I was a soldier with the King in the Holy Land; but more than that, I was the King's armorer. With these hands I made the King of England's sword, the sword that cut great swathes through the Saracen hordes. Oh, my King, my King!" And he began to weep, burying his head in his hands.

Robin and Much and Tuck looked at each other and smiled. "Friend," Robin began, "did you say you were an armorer? A smith?"

The man nodded behind his hands.

Tuck crossed himself and closed his eyes. "Now, God be thanked," he breathed. "Didn't I tell you, Robin? Didn't I now? It's God's good grace that has brought him here."

Robin pulled the man's hands gently from his face. "Friend, come live with us in Sherwood, make our swords for us, sharpen our spears; and then we can deal Prince John the usurper and the Sheriff of Nottingham such a blow as they'll never forget. Do it for the King."

The stranger smiled through his tears. "So," he said, "so the spirit of England still lives. I'll stay, and I'll make you all the daggers and swords and shields and spears you need to clear the vermin from King Richard's land."

"What shall we call you?" Robin asked.

"My name is John Little, but my King always called me Little John because I was twice his size. Call me that, for it will always remind me of him when you do."

Through that autumn and winter Little John's forge was never cold. By Christmas every man, woman, and child had his or her own weapon, each one perfectly weighted and deadly sharp. The children loved to watch him at work on his anvil, to see the sparks fly and the gush of steam rise as he plunged the

glowing iron into the bucket. It was the warmest place to be, too, and they would stay and listen long into the night as Little John told them of the Holy Land, and of the wars he had fought alongside good King Richard.

Christmas that year was like no other. All through the feasting, they knew their time of testing was coming, that for many of them, this might be the last Christmas. The Outcast band had swelled now to more than two hundred, all of them strong in body and spirit, all of them ready to fight the good fight. Mass was the longest they had ever known, partly because much time was given over to Friar Tuck's exhortations, and partly because he had insisted that it was high time for all couples to be married and their children blessed in the sight of God.

Last of all to be joined together were Robin and Marion. As they knelt for the blessing, Tuck prayed over them.

"God's good grace brought you together, and brought us all to this place. May you and your children, and all of us, live a long and a godly life."

The *amen*s echoed loudly through the cave; and afterward, the Christmas feasting went on long into the night, though Robin and Marion stole away well before the end of it.

"Will our baby have white hair like me, or black like you?" Marion whispered as they lay together in each other's arms.

"It does not matter," said Robin. "So long as he grows up a free man, nothing else matters."

"Well, I want him to have white hair so that when he grows old no one will ever know it. And anyway, we don't know—he may be a girl."

But Robin did not hear. He was asleep already.

The baby was born as the first leaves of autumn fell, a baby boy. And Marion's wish came true. The boy had white hair. He was baptized Martin, after his grandfather.

SEVEN

The Silver Arrow

All this while, Sir Guy of Gisbourne had not been idle. He was gathering evidence, evidence to prove that Robin Hood was still alive. He was convinced of it, so convinced that he would never have dared to venture into Sherwood himself. Word from his spies had left no doubt in his mind. Robin Hood was gathering about him in Sherwood a small army of malcontents and rebels. True, no one had actually seen Robin Hood in person for three years or more now, and in all that time no one had robbed travelers on the road through Sherwood. But the stories about Robin and his Outcasts had spread like the plague, into every back street, into every tavern. Sir Guy had heard it with his own ears. One man, about to die at the end of a rope, declared with absolute conviction: "Robin will avenge us!" And then died, defiant with faith, his eyes burning with it until they closed in death. Those eyes haunted Sir Guy of Gisbourne.

Robin the Good, they called him. Saint Robin, Sheriff of Sherwood. To some he was a friendly sprite, a Jack o' the green, a part of the living forest; to others he was dead indeed, but like Jesus Christ before him he would come back to save them. There was even a rumor that Robin Hood was the true son of the imprisoned King Richard, and so heir to the English throne.

What Sir Guy of Gisbourne knew for certain was frightening enough. Robin Hood lived. He was a bowman without equal in the land. He could split a willow wand at five hundred paces. He could do it every time, wind or rain. And the Outcasts in Sherwood would follow him anywhere. Worst of all, and most dangerous of all, the people loved him.

Time and again Sir Guy of Gisbourne tried to persuade the Sheriff that Robin Hood was still alive. Every stag's head Guy's men found, he threw down at the Sheriff's feet. "I tell you, my lord Sheriff," he insisted yet again, "he lives. He has followers, maybe hundreds of them by now, and he has weapons. He will come against us with his Outcasts; and when he does, none of us will be safe in our beds."

But the Sheriff had had enough. "What in hell's name is the matter with you, Guy?" he stormed. "We've seen neither hide nor hair of the man in years. All you have is stories, tavern tittle-tattle, and a few stags' heads. Anyone can kill a stag."

"But, my lord Sheriff—"

"No *buts*." The Sheriff banged the table and leaped to his feet in a terrible rage. "I've listened enough to your *buts*. Have you once been into the forest to look for him? No, of course you haven't. You're gutless, gutless. I am surrounded by cowards and imbeciles. I'll show you! I'll show you! To prove to you once and for all that I am right, that Robin Hood is dead, and dead as a doornail, I shall go myself into Sherwood; and what's more, I shall go alone. And after I return, if anyone, *anyone*, even speaks the name of Robin Hood again in my hearing, I'll have his tongue out. Do you hear me?" And snatching up his sword and helmet, he strode out of the hall, leaped onto his horse, and galloped away over the drawbridge.

In the market square the Sheriff's escorts made as if to mount up and come after him, but he waved them back. "I do not need you, nor anyone," he thundered. "I ride through Sherwood alone. I am not frightened of a ghost— not Robin Hood's, not anyone's." So they let him go.

But his last words had been heard by everyone in the market square, including a charcoal-burner whose family had been put out of their house by the Sheriff and were only kept alive through the cold months of winter by Robin and his Outcasts. This man knew what had to be done and was more than happy to do it.

The sun was high and hot by the time the Sheriff reached the shade of Sherwood. Glad though he was to be in the cool again, the Sheriff had no intention of staying in Sherwood any longer than he had to. Never in his life had he ventured alone into Sherwood, even before the days of Robin Hood. For Robin Hood was not the only danger lurking in Sherwood; deep in the forest there were wolves, too.

And then, his temper cooled at last, a sudden terrible thought came to the Sheriff. Maybe, just maybe, he had been wrong. Maybe Robin Hood was still alive after all, still there in Sherwood. He reined in his horse at once and looked anxiously about him. This was far enough. He would hide himself in among the trees for an hour or two and then ride back in triumph to Nottingham. Neither Sir Guy of Gisbourne nor anyone would ever know the difference. He led his horse into a thicket, tied it up, and sat down to sleep off his lunch. He had had two bottles of wine, so sleep came easily enough.

When he woke he found himself surrounded by peering, grinning faces, a dozen or more. Some were dwarfs, and there were cagots and hunchbacks, too—but not dressed in rags, as he remembered them. Each one wore the same Lincoln green and each one carried a sword, a bow, and a quiver of arrows. The Sheriff knew at once they were the Outcasts and shrank back in horror.

"We won't kill you," said one of them, smiling from ear to ear. "We've been sent to ask you for supper. Will Scarlett killed a stag, a beauty, a real beauty. We kept it for a special occasion. You're the special occasion." They helped him to his feet.

"I think I'd better be getting back," said the Sheriff, backing away; but they held him fast.

"After supper, perhaps," said the same Outcast, looking up into his face. "We wouldn't want to disappoint our master, now, would we? We're cooking it specially for you."

The Sheriff had no choice but to brave it out. "Very well, then, but who is your master?" he asked, dreading the answer; for he knew it already.

"You'll know soon enough," the Outcast replied with a laugh. "He's been longing to meet you. We all have, haven't we, lads?" And the Sheriff looked at the faces of his laughing captors and hoped that death would at least be quick.

They blindfolded him and led him away, none too gently, into the forest. Robin and the Outcasts were gathered in eager anticipation around the fire. They had scarcely been able to believe their good fortune when the charcoal-burner had brought the news that the Sheriff of Nottingham would be riding alone into Sherwood to prove once and for all that Robin Hood was dead. Friar Tuck pronounced at length upon how God was delivering their enemy into their hands, and while they were waiting everyone sat about devising ever more gruesome ways of killing the Sheriff, of "butchering the butcher." Every new bloodthirsty suggestion was greeted with another resounding cheer. But after a while Robin went away and sat silent, alone under his tree. As much as anyone else around the fire, he, too, had reason enough to hate the Sheriff of Nottingham; yet even so, he could not bring himself to gloat at the prospect of the man's death. He just wanted it done and over with. He still had not made up his mind how it should be done when a great hush fell around the fire and he saw the Sheriff being led toward him.

"Take off his blindfold," said Robin. "Let me look at him."

It was a face fat with good living. The little piggy eyes that looked back at him were darting with terror.

"You are Robin Hood?" the Sheriff breathed.

"I am, and alive, too, as you see."

The Sheriff dropped to his knees. "I will give you all I have, everything. Only, in God's holy name, spare my life."

"Like you spared my father's eyes?" said Robin.

"That was Guy of Gisbourne, it was his idea."

Robin drew his sword and raised it high above his head. "You miserable worm!" he cried. "I hope you wriggle at both ends when I cut you in half."

But Marion held him by the arm. "Do not do it, Robin," she said. "It will not bring your father's sight back, nor Much's father, nor will it right the thousand wrongs the Sheriff has done us all. Punish him, yes; but do not kill him. I do not want our son to have an executioner for a father. Have mercy, Robin; show this wicked man how to have mercy."

Robin looked down at the pathetic figure prostrating itself at his feet and suddenly felt nothing but pity.

"Please, Robin," whispered Marion. "For me."

Robin sheathed his sword and lifted the Sheriff to his feet. "Tonight, Sheriff," he began, "you will sup with us off the King's deer, King Richard's deer. If it doesn't

choke you, and I pray it will, then you may leave with your wretched life, but everything else we will take."

So the Sheriff sat down with the Outcasts and was obliged to eat the King's venison with them. As the ale flowed, the Outcasts became wilder and wilder in their boisterous celebrations, lampooning the Sheriff to his face and cursing him roundly, as well as Sir Guy of Gisbourne and Prince John and anyone else who came to mind. At Little John's suggestion, they drank a defiant toast to the return of good King Richard, Richard the Lionheart; and death to the usurper, Prince John. The Sheriff had no alternative but to drink along with them. All the while, Much looked on in silence, his eyes never leaving the Sheriff's face.

"Well," said Robin, merry with ale now, "what do you think, Sheriff? Will you become one of us? Will you live in the forest and sleep on the good earth, as we do? As you see, we live well enough, and we shall live better, too. From this day until the return of the King we shall rob all we can. We shall use all we need for the poor, and the rest we shall save for good King Richard's ransom. We shall have our King back, Sheriff. We will not rest until we do. Stay with us, redeem yourself, and you can keep all you have. Go, and we shall take everything. Well?"

"Let me go, I beg you," the Sheriff pleaded, still fearful for his life. "Let me go and I shall leave you in peace to do what you like, rob who you like, I promise."

"Your promises," said Robin, "are like dead wood, brittle, too easily broken, and full of rot. I have given you your chance. Now go. But first take off your clothes, all of them, every stitch of them."

So, to the rapturous delight of the Outcasts, the Sheriff of Nottingham was set upon his horse, naked as the day he was born; and Robin and Much, the miller's son, led him away into the darkness of the forest with the Outcasts' laughter ringing in their ears. When they reached the road to Nottingham, Robin slapped the horse's rump and sent the shivering Sheriff galloping off home.

"You should have let me hang him, Robin. You promised me," said Much quietly. Robin said nothing, for there was nothing he could say. He knew that Much was right, and he knew in his heart that Marion had been right as well.

"Let's get home, Much," said Robin. "Father'll be telling Martin his bedtime story. He tells them just like he always did, word for word. I like listening to them. It makes me feel like a child again."

"We should have killed him," said Much, but after that he never spoke of it again.

They heard it first from a merchant they robbed. No one really believed it. It seemed just too obvious. Then Tuck came back from one of his frequent pilgrimages with the evidence of it in his hand, a notice he had torn down from a church door. It read:

Who is the finest bowman in England? A contest will be held on May Day at Nottingham. A silver arrow and a hundred pounds to the champion.

The notices were everywhere, Tuck told them. Town criers shouted the challenge from every market square in the land. People talked of little else. The contest would be held beneath the city walls, and the Sheriff of Nottingham himself would give away the prize.

It was a trap. All the Outcasts knew it. Robin knew it. The Sheriff knew they would know it. What he counted on was Robin's audacity. Ever since his humiliating ride naked through the streets of Nottingham, the Sheriff had planned and plotted together with Sir Guy of Gisbourne how to dispose of Robin Hood. To go into Sherwood after him would be suicidal. Somehow they had to tempt him out into the open, him and his Outcasts, and then destroy them.

All through April, the Sheriff and Sir Guy of Gisbourne worked on their plan. They would leave nothing to chance—bowmen on the city walls above the butts; horsemen mounted and ready for pursuit, hidden away in the back streets; and encircling the crowd, watching and waiting, three hundred men-at-arms. If Robin Hood did come, he would never leave alive.

All through April, Marion begged Robin not to go, but this time Robin would not be persuaded. "Didn't I listen once before?" he said. "And now the Sheriff plays cat-and-mouse with me, and the world knows it. I have to go, I will go, and I will bring back the silver arrow for you and for Martin. Do not try to stop me."

"Then at least let us come with you," she pleaded with him.

"Don't you see?" said Robin. "That is just what they expect, just what they hope for. No, I stand a better chance with just Much and Tuck and Little John. We'll go alone, and that's the end of it."

And Marion knew then that there was no hope of stopping him.

The morning of the contest dawned misty, but by the time the sun came through, the meadow below the city walls was filled with the best bowmen from all over England. They came from as far north as Northumbria, as far west as Cornwall. By four o'clock that afternoon the crowd had swelled to several thousand, and there were only twenty bowmen left in the contest. From the ramparts above, the Sheriff and Sir Guy scrutinized these last twenty, but with hoods up to shield their eyes from the sun, their faces could not be seen clearly. There was a friar in among the bowmen, and a great bear of a man with a russet beard. The Sheriff thought he recognized both from his visit to Sherwood but he could not be sure. What was certain was that neither one was Robin Hood. The friar was too fat and the bearded man too tall. They would bide their time. Robin Hood would be among the others, and like as not he would win. The Sheriff was counting on it. And when the champion came up to the ramparts to collect the silver arrow, then they would spring the trap.

The bowmen stood farther and farther from their targets now, and the huge crowd hushed as each one of them drew his bow and shot. Wand after wand was split. Wand after wand was missed.

They were down to the last three now, the friar, the bearded giant, and a slight young man who the Sheriff was now quite sure must be Robin Hood himself.

"Take him now," whispered Sir Guy, "while you can. Give the order."

"No," said the Sheriff. "We'd have a riot on our hands. Let's keep to the plan. Let him come up for his prize and we shall have him."

First the friar failed, at six hundred paces. Then the giant's arrow hit the wand but did not split it.

The young man stepped coolly forward and raised his bow and fired his arrow. It split the wand clean in two.

A great cheer went up, and despite all the Sheriff's men could do, the crowd surged forward and surrounded the young man. He was at once hoisted up and

carried away shoulder high, away from the city walls, away from the Sheriff. When Much, the miller's son (for that was who was carrying him), set Robin down on his feet again, the Sheriff lost sight of him in the mêlée.

The Sheriff gripped the walls with fury as he realized what was happening. He saw the friar being swept along in the crowd, but of Robin Hood there was no sign at all. He was one of the crowd now, and indistinguishable from anyone else. The Sheriff raged and stormed, but no one heard him except Sir Guy of Gisbourne, who had suddenly noticed two riders beyond the crowd, galloping hard for the forest.

There was still a chance to catch him. They raced down the steps, leaped onto their horses, and clattered out through the city gates, calling for their waiting horsemen to follow them.

Robin and Much would have made it back to Sherwood with ease, except for the badger's hole. As they neared the forest, their pursuers in sight but a safe distance behind, Robin's horse shied at a rising buzzard, leaped a ditch, and careered off into a field. Robin hung on, but when the horse trod in a badger's hole and stumbled, Robin came off, twisting his leg under him as he landed. He heard the excited, triumphant yell of the Sheriff's men and saw Much riding to his help. He tried to stand and couldn't. Then Much was beside him, his sword drawn, putting himself between Robin and the Sheriff's men.

There was no time to mount Much's horse. They would have to stand and fight. "Help me up, Much!" Robin cried. "Let me shoot off one arrow, one arrow for the Sheriff."

"Your horn, Robin!" shouted Much, against the thunder of the oncoming hooves. "Blow your horn!"

Robin put his horn to his lips and blew. But no one came, and the horsemen were so close by now that he could see their eyes. Then, with a war yell that sent shivers down every spine, the Outcasts came pouring out of the forest. Like a rush of starlings overhead, the arrows flew over Much and Robin and into the charging horsemen. Most fell at that first volley. The rest were speared from their saddles, and once on the ground they were finished off with sword and dagger.

It was a brutal and terrible fight but, mercifully, quickly over. Sir Guy of Gisbourne rode from the field with an arrow in his thigh; and the Sheriff, still unscathed, went with him. Barely half a dozen of the hundred who rode out of Nottingham that day survived.

But every victory has its price. For the first time, the Outcasts had lost men and women in battle. They carried the bodies home to the encampment that evening,

and while all the talk was of how they had faced the Sheriff's men in open combat and beaten them, there was no rejoicing. Robin sat with Marion under his tree, little Martin on his good knee, and was glad to be alive. It had been a near thing. But his leg throbbed with pain, and with every minute that passed he was becoming more anxious. Neither Tuck nor Little John had come home from Nottingham and it was getting late.

As the shadows lengthened that evening, neither Robin nor anyone else dared voice their fears, for they all knew well enough what would happen to Tuck and Little John, had they been captured.

At last Robin could not stand it any longer. "I can't just sit here," he said. "I have to go back and find out what's happened to them."

But Will Scarlett spoke up strongly. "We have six dead already, Robin. Is that not enough? Go back into Nottingham, and you won't come back alive. If they are taken, then we need you here with us, not hanging alongside them on a rope."

Not long afterward, Robin was limping up and down, kicking at the embers and cursing himself, when Friar Tuck came sauntering out of the trees and into the light of the fire. "Well!" Tuck cried. "Have you ever seen such long faces! Don't look at me like that. I'm not a ghost just yet, by God's good grace."

Robin hugged him as if he would never let go. "Little John?" he asked. "Where's Little John?"

"He'll be along," said Tuck. "He just stopped for a piddle. Too much ale—he can't hold it, the old goat, not like I can, by God's good grace. After we heard about the mauling you'd all given the Sheriff and Sir Guy of Gisbourne, we went and had a little drink or two to celebrate."

"Robin!" boomed a voice from behind him. It was Little John. "So you made it. I told Tuck you would, didn't I, Tuck? They won't get him, I said; they never do."

"Where've you been?" Robin said. "You had me worried sick."

"Here"—and Little John held out the arrow with the glinting silver arrowhead. "The Sheriff left your prize behind when he went after you. So, seeing as he didn't seem to want it, we took it. Oh yes," he went on, shaking a purse in Robin's face, "and this, too. The hundred pounds the Sheriff owed you, your prize money. You won it, remember?"

"So I did," said Robin, running his hands along the arrow. "Here's one arrow I'll never shoot in anger." And with that he gave it to Marion, just as he had promised he would. "For you and little Martin. Keep it always with you, Marion. It'll be our talisman and a token of our love."

They buried their dead the next day, in the clearing beyond the encampment. As the bodies were lowered into their graves, Friar Tuck blessed each one; and when it was all over closed his eyes in prayer. "May the good Lord love them and keep them in His good grace. And may He deliver us from the beast of Nottingham; for the beast is only wounded, and the wounds will heal. Give us the strength, Lord, to finish what we have begun." And everyone cried "Amen!" to that.

For some months afterward there was an uneasy peace. Every day the Outcasts expected an attack, but none came, and in time they began to hope, and then to believe, that none would ever come. They felt safe again. Even Robin dared hope that they had done enough, that they had seen the last of the Sheriff of Nottingham.

He was wrong. They were all wrong.

Back in the castle at Nottingham, the Sheriff sat day after day staring blankly into the fire, still so enraged that no one but Sir Guy of Gisbourne dared speak to him. Every scheme for revenge that Sir Guy came up with, he dismissed out of hand, until one evening in late summer. Sir Guy, quite recovered now from his wound, was sharpening his sword. Suddenly he stopped.

"I have it!" he cried. "There is a way."

The Sheriff, still sunk in his humiliation, said nothing.

"Didn't you tell me he has a son?"

"So?"

"What if somehow we were to spirit him away? Robin would be bound to come after him, wouldn't he?"

The Sheriff looked up. "You mean kidnap him?"

"Why not? We could bring the child back here. What father would not try to save his son? And we'd be waiting for him."

The Sheriff sprang to his feet. "Yes!" he cried. "Yes! But how? How do we do it?"

"Leave it to me, my lord Sheriff," said Sir Guy of Gisbourne, a weasel smile twisting his lip. "I shall ride tomorrow to your sister, the Abbess of Kirkleigh. I have an idea she might be able to help us. It may take a while, my lord Sheriff, but this time I will bring you Robin Hood; that much I promise you. Upon my life I promise it. Would you like his head on a plate like John the Baptist's?"

"Alive," the Sheriff hissed through clenched jaws. "I want Robin Hood alive."

EIGHT

The Sheriff's Revenge

There was only one road from London to the north, and it ran through Sherwood for twenty miles. So for twenty miles every traveler had to run the gauntlet of Robin Hood and his Outcasts. They never laid an ambush in the same place twice, and they picked their targets carefully, too. The poor had nothing to fear. Indeed, it was not at all uncommon for a beggar to find himself invited for supper with Robin and his Outcasts and then be sent on his way the next morning with a suit of warm clothes and enough money to live on for a year. But for the rich and powerful, the journey through Sherwood was always hazardous. They sought protection in numbers, passing through in great convoys of carts and carriages, armed escorts to the front, and more bringing up the rear. It did them little good.

As far as the Outcasts were concerned, the bigger the convoy the better. There was rarely much resistance and, so, little need for killing. They would block the road ahead of the convoy and behind it with fallen trees, and then simply drop on them out of nowhere. The rich, too, would be invited to share a meal of the King's venison around the fire; but Robin would invite them to pay for their dinner, unlike the poor. The price was always the same, half of what they had. But if they ever lied about the amount of money or jewels or cloth they were carrying—and they often did—then Robin would take everything they owned before setting them on their way again, his last words ringing in their ears: "And do not worry, my friend, your money will be used wisely. The homeless will have homes again, the hungry will be fed, the have-nots will have. And tell the Sheriff this—tell Prince John if you like—that we will soon have enough saved to pay the good King Richard's ransom. The people will have their rightful King back home, and soon."

Every time the Sheriff heard this, it sent him into paroxysms of rage and fear, in about equal parts. He taunted Sir Guy of Gisbourne with his promise, but Sir Guy would not be baited. He told the Sheriff to be patient, that for his plan to

work Robin and his Outcasts must be lulled into a sense of false security, which would take time. "Never fear, my lord Sheriff, it won't be long now," he promised again and again.

But the weeks passed, and the months; and still Robin Hood was at large, and every day more and more the people's hero. Each new story of how he had robbed the rich to give to the poor, or of some small kindness, was turning the man into a living legend. Exasperated, the Sheriff sent for help to Prince John again, but the Prince was busy with other rebellions and could not or would not spare the Sheriff any more soldiers. The Sheriff was at his wits' end. Once King Richard's ransom was paid, he knew it would be the end of him. Somehow Robin Hood had to be stopped. Somehow.

These were good times in Sherwood. More and more people flocked to Robin's cause, happy enough to endure the hardships of living in the forest so long as they had the opportunity to fight the Sheriff and Sir Guy of Gisbourne. Friar Tuck made Christians of them whether they liked it or not—and he was not a gentle persuader. Between him and Much and Robin, they made soldiers of them. Marion welcomed them all with open arms to their new home in Sherwood; she would turn no one away. But Will Scarlett and Robin's father were not so pleased to see this new influx. They both knew how easy it would be to plant a spy in their camp. And they were right, too, but Robin would not listen.

Among those who had recently joined was a cobbler from Nottingham, one Alan Wicken. His hand had been chopped off, he told them, by the Sheriff himself, in punishment for rent he could not pay. They had no reason to doubt him. What neither Robin nor anyone else could know was that he had lost his hand in a drunken brawl in London, and that he was a spy in the pay of Guy of Gisbourne. Alan Wicken was to let him know when next Friar Tuck was away on pilgrimage, for the friar was the only one who knew the Abbess of Kirkleigh by sight and could betray her. He was also to make particular friends with Marion, and more importantly, much more importantly, to ingratiate himself with little Martin. It was not difficult; for Marion, even more than Robin, was the kind who always liked to think the best of anyone. Alan would play for hours on end with little Martin. No one saw any harm in that.

Friar Tuck had gone away on pilgrimage to Canterbury, and Alan had got word of it to Sir Guy as quickly as he could. He was romping with little Martin when Little John and Much came into the encampment, escorting a poor Abbess and a dozen or more ragged-looking nuns. Robin and Marion greeted each of them warmly and invited them to share their supper that evening. They ate ravenously,

as only poor people do. Like everyone, Robin could see from their patched and torn habits and their bare, bleeding feet that these were not among those many nuns and friars who lived so well off the backs of the poor and needy.

"Eat all you want," he said, overcome with pity. "Stay as long as you like. Will Scarlett here will make you new habits. He has the cloth. He always has the cloth. He made all this green we stand up in, every stitch of it, didn't you, Will? . . . You shall have shoes on your feet. Alan Wicken will see to it for you. And then with good food inside you, you will soon be strong enough again to do God's work, which is so much needed in this benighted land of ours."

"May God bless you, good Robin Hood," said the Abbess. "I see that all we have heard about you is true." And with that she hung her head and began to sob uncontrollably. "Our dear abbey has been plundered. Sir Guy of Gisbourne deceived us, took all we had. It was our fault, but it was cruel, cruel. We needed money, so we mortgaged the abbey. We had to. The church roof was falling in. We had to save it. We had to try, didn't we?"

"Of course," said Marion, taking her hand to comfort her.

"Two bad harvests, and we could not pay Sir Guy back his money," the Abbess went on. "So he took it, took the abbey from us and put us out."

"I wonder sometimes," said Robin fiercely, "I wonder which of them Satan loves more, the Sheriff or Sir Guy of Gisbourne."

"You shall stay here with us," Marion declared, "all of you. You can help teach the children to read and to write."

"May we really stay?" cried the Abbess, falling on her knees. "Oh, thank you, sweet Jesus, for your mercy. My sisters and I, we shall sing mass for you. We can heal, too, with the help of the sweet Lord Jesus. I know more of the herbs of this forest than anyone alive."

"Marion is our healer." Little John spoke sharply. "And Friar Tuck says mass for us. He's away at the moment, on a pilgrimage to Canterbury, but he'll be back."

"Then we shall sing the services for you until he returns," said the Abbess, smiling sweetly. "Meanwhile, my sisters and I will teach the children, and only if Marion wishes it will we help her with the healing of the sick."

"I need all the help I can get," said Marion, wondering why Little John had a face like thunder.

So the Abbess and the nuns stayed among the Outcasts, ministering to the sick, teaching the children, and singing mass in the cave chapel each day. And Will Scarlett and Alan Wicken worked all the daylight hours, making them their new habits and new sandals.

Among all the Outcasts, only Little John did not welcome them. He confided his doubts to Robin. "They're just too good to be true," he said. "Not natural."

Robin brushed him aside. "Nonsense," he said. "You worry too much. The Abbess cured my father's aching leg when Marion couldn't. And when they sing mass, even the birds listen. When Tuck does it you can't see a bird or beast for half a mile all around."

"I don't like her. I don't like any of them," Little John insisted, but Robin paid him little attention.

Some weeks later, it was Little John himself, on lookout duty on the edge of Sherwood, who spotted the approaching convoy. Word came back that it was southward bound, and a big one—at least thirty carts, with only a light escort. Rich pickings, easy pickings.

"We'll need everyone," said Robin.

"We'll look after the children for you, Marion," said the Abbess. "They'll be fine with us."

Alan Wicken would stay behind, to finish a sandal, he said. And Robin's father stayed, too—he rarely left the encampment. Marion said she would stay with him as she so often did, but he wouldn't hear of it. "You go with Robin," he said. "I'll be

all right here with the sisters and Alan. Little Martin will look after me." And she left him fashioning a longbow, lifting it to his nose as he whittled, and smelling the yew, his grandson crawling in the leaves at his feet.

Alan Wicken waited until everyone was gone, until the Abbess gave him the signal he had been waiting for.

It had all been planned, and planned perfectly, too. He sauntered over to Robin's father. "Some of the sisters want to go looking for herbs," he said. "They're taking the children. I'd best go with them, keep an eye on them. Shall I take young Martin with us? Let you whittle in peace?"

"Why not? You take good care of him, mind you."

"Oh, I will," said Alan Wicken. "I most certainly will." But Robin's father could not see the smirk on his face as he picked up the child and walked away.

The ambush proved to be a bitter disappointment. For some reason the Outcasts could not understand, the convoy seemed to change its mind before it even reached Sherwood. Frustrated and furious, the Outcasts could only watch helpless from the trees as the convoy turned and made its way back toward Nottingham. They returned to the encampment to find Robin's father stumbling around, distraught and calling for his grandson.

The Abbess was gone. The nuns were gone, and so was little Martin Hood. The other children were found some way off, playing by a stream, but Martin was not among them. The Outcasts searched through the forest but he was nowhere to be seen.

If Little John had not stopped him and Much had not pinned him to the ground, Robin would have gone after Martin at once.

"Don't you see, Robin?" cried Little John. "That is exactly what they want you to do. It's a trap. The whole thing is a trap."

"He's right," said Will Scarlett. "They tempted us away, all of us, and we fell for it."

"It was Alan Wicken!" Robin's father cried in his grief and in his shame. "I let him walk with the child. It was my fault."

"Not so," said Marion, wiping the tears from her face. "He is my child. It is my fault. It is a mother's duty to care for her child, and I left him. No one will go after him except me. It was I who brought all this upon you, Robin. If you had killed the Sheriff when you had him at your mercy, then none of this would have happened. And who more than anyone welcomed in those devilish sisters? I did. The blame is mine, all mine. So it is all mine to put right." She turned to Will Scarlett. "Will, I need to look as they looked. Can you make me a habit by morning?"

Nothing Robin nor anyone else could say would deter her. "They'll have taken him to Nottingham," she said. "They are expecting you to come after him, Robin. They will not be expecting me. We have surprise on our side. And haven't you told me and told me that in war—and this is war—surprise is everything?"

All night long, as Will Scarlett worked on her nun's habit, Marion talked through her plan with Robin. At dawn, she gathered everyone around her and told them what she had in mind. It was left to Much to pick the precise place, for he knew more than anyone every fold of the land around the mill.

Robin listened but found it difficult to concentrate. All he could think of was little Martin and what the Sheriff might do to him, might have done to him already.

"It'll work, Robin," said Marion, taking him by the shoulder. "It's the only way. And timing is everything. They must see no one but you. Do not move until you see me wave the silver arrow. May God help us bring him home safe."

Once on the road to Nottingham, Marion and Robin held each other close, neither wanting to let the other go, for both knew just how much depended on these next few hours.

Robin tried to make light of it. "I've never hugged a nun before," he said. "Keep your eyes lowered in Nottingham. They must not see your eyes."

"If Tuck were here he'd tell us to have faith," she said; and gathering her nun's habit about her, she mounted her horse and rode off. "Don't be late," she called out. And with a wave of the silver arrow, she was gone.

At noon that day a nun, her head lowered in prayer, rode in through the gates of Nottingham and up through little back streets into the market square. No one paid her the slightest attention. Everyone was far too busy buying and selling to even notice her. She dismounted and led her horse over the castle drawbridge and into the courtyard beyond. She handed the reins to one of the Sheriff's men standing by the well. "I must see the Sheriff," she said. "I have a message for him from Robin Hood."

She was led at once into the great hall of the castle, and there before her stood the Sheriff with Sir Guy of Gisbourne beside him. She ran toward them and fell on her knees, her hands together in supplication. "My lord Sheriff, you have my son." And she pulled back her wimple to show her face. "You know me, my lord Sheriff."

"Robin Hood's woman," smirked the Sheriff.

"As you say, Robin Hood's woman; but no longer. I will give you his head, my lord, in exchange for my son."

"It's a trick," Sir Guy of Gisbourne scoffed, drawing his sword. But the Sheriff held him back.

"Maybe," said the Sheriff, walking around Marion as she knelt, her eyes pleading. "And maybe not. The disguise? Why the disguise?"

"I am a cagot, an albino, as you see, my lord. I am an Outcast. Could I have got even through the city gates without a disguise?"

"True enough," said the Sheriff.

"And I suppose," sneered Sir Guy of Gisbourne, "I suppose you will lead us to him—no doubt deep in Sherwood, where we shall be ambushed. What do you imagine we are, imbeciles?"

"No, my lord," said Marion, and she drew from under her habit the silver arrow. "You know this arrow, I think. I have only to wave it and he is yours. He waits for me by the burned-out mill, in open country, my lord. And he waits alone. But he will not show himself until he sees me with the child. The silver arrow is a signal. I wave it above my head and he knows all is well, that I have rescued the child and brought him out safely. All you have to do is follow me, at a safe distance

and unseen, and he is yours to do with what you will. I will have my only son and you will have Robin Hood."

"A trick, I tell you!" cried Sir Guy of Gisbourne. "A trick."

"Sometimes, Guy," said the Sheriff scornfully, "sometimes I think you are a very stupid man. You send my sister into Sherwood to bring out the child so that Robin Hood will come after him. She does it. We have the child. So Robin Hood may not have come himself, as you thought he would, but his woman has. And the result will be the same—Robin Hood's head. Do you know how strong is a woman's love for her child? No. She would do nothing to risk her son's life. She would do anything to save him, anything. Look at her. Take my word for it, she will lead us to him. Have no doubt of it, for she knows what will happen to the child if she does not."

"She will lead us into a trap!" Sir Guy roared. "Can't you see it? I see in those scheming red eyes nothing of motherly love, but only revenge and hate."

"Bring me the child," the Sheriff called out. "And have three hundred men ready, armed, and on foot at the south gate." He smiled at Sir Guy. "You forget, Guy, that the wheat is high in the fields. I shall hide my men in the wheat. No one will see them. She will ride ahead with her son, wave the silver arrow; and we will

wait. If he comes, we shall kill him. If he does not, then we shall know it is a trick and we shall kill her and the child. What have we to lose?"

At this moment the door opened and the Abbess of Kirkleigh came into the room, carrying little Martin in her arms, Alan Wicken alongside her. The child reached out for his mother, but the Abbess held him tight and listened in silence, her eyes fixed on Marion and dark with suspicion, as the Sheriff told her how at last they would capture Robin Hood, led to him by his own woman.

"Brother," she said, "do not do it. Do not give the child to this woman. I know her. She loves Robin Hood better than life itself."

"And maybe she loves her son more," retorted the Sheriff. "What do you know of a woman's love? What do you know of a mother's love?"

"Listen to her, my lord," said Alan Wicken. "She is right. I have seen the love in her eyes. She would never betray him, not in a million years."

"Do you think I haven't thought of all this?" stormed the Sheriff, snatching the child away and handing him to Marion.

She cuddled him and kissed him, the tears running down her cheeks. "Thank you, my Lord, thank you." And Marion put up her wimple again. "You are right, both of you," she said. "Yes, I love my Robin, and I hate what I am about to do; but my child comes before anything, before anyone." And with the boy in her arms

she walked out of the great hall of the castle, set him on the saddle of her horse, and mounted up behind him.

Robin and Much and Little John lay in the dry ditch by the burned-out mill. "I should never have let her do it," Robin was saying, and not for the first time. "It's madness. Does she think a nun's habit will protect her? What if the Sheriff doesn't go along with it? What if he takes her prisoner, too? What if he kills them both?"

"What if? What if?" said Little John, chewing on some barleycorn. "Did you think 'what if' when you went in there to rescue your father? Well, did you?"

"If she's not here soon," said Robin, "I'm going in after her."

"You won't need to," whispered Much, who was peering over the top of the ditch. "Have a look." And there over the crest of the hill Marion came riding, little Martin clinging to the pommel of the saddle and bouncing up and down.

Robin squinted into the sun. "Are you sure it's Marion?"

"It's Marion right enough," said Little John, his hand grasping Robin's arm. "But wait for her signal like she said."

As they watched, they saw Marion rein the horse to a standstill. Then she was waving the arrow in the air, the silver glinting in the sun. "Up you go, then, Robin," said Little John. Robin leaped out of the ditch and ran down the road, past the burned-out mill. As planned, he slowed to a walk as he climbed the hill. The wheat was high in the fields all around him. She let him come on as long as she dared, then all of a sudden put her heels to her horse's side and came galloping down toward him, one arm around little Martin.

Behind her, from the wheat on both sides of the road, rose an army of the Sheriff's men. Robin lifted his horn to his lips and blew. His own army of Outcasts,

some five hundred strong now, rose as one from the standing wheat and at once let loose five hundred arrows, none at random, each one aimed at a man's heart.

Scores of the Sheriff's men fell back into the wheat, some ran at once, and the rest stood their ground as the Outcasts came at them, their bloodcurdling war yell on the air, their great swords scything both wheat and men before them.

Marion and the child rode through the oncoming Outcasts, on to Sherwood and safety. But Robin, Much, and Little John stood shoulder to shoulder with the Outcasts and fought. This was no short, sharp ambush, no little skirmish. This was a vicious close-quarter killing battle.

Each Outcast hacked and slashed until the man in front of him dropped, and when he did, there always seemed to be another to take his place. They were all of them wet with blood and sweat, and tears, too.

All those lessons Tuck and Much and Robin had taught them stood them in good stead, for after two hours' fighting the Sheriff's men at last turned and ran.

From the top of the hill the Sheriff and Sir Guy of Gisbourne watched all this in horror and disbelief. Neither dared even to draw his sword, for both knew that they would surely be sought out by the Outcasts and die in the wheat that afternoon if ever they joined the battle. As their men streamed past them toward Nottingham, battered and bleeding in defeat, they saw the triumphant Outcasts simply melt away into the wheat again, a phantom army disappearing.

Over two hundred lay dead in the wheat that night when Robin and his Outcasts came back to collect their dead. They knew already who was missing, whom to look for. Thirty-five of them had died in the fierce heat of the battle that afternoon, thirty-five good friends, thirty-five good fighters the band could ill afford to lose. They carried the bodies back home to Sherwood and buried them in the clearing with the others.

Little Martin was safely home, and the battle had been won; but grief is a more powerful thing than exultation. The Outcasts lay down that night on the forest floor, numb in their sadness but thankful they were still alive to see the stars above them.

In Nottingham Castle the Sheriff brooded by his fire and swore that he would hang, draw, and quarter anyone who was ever heard to speak the name of Robin Hood. Side by side in bed that night, Sir Guy of Gisbourne and the Abbess of Kirkleigh swore they would not rest until the day Robin Hood lay dead and cold in his grave.

NINE

RICHARD The LIONHEART

 When Friar Tuck returned from his pilgrimage a few days later, he was not alone. The wan young man he brought with him seemed sunk in a deep sadness. He stared about in bewilderment as the Outcasts crowded around him.

"Who are you? Who is he, Tuck?" they asked.

Friar Tuck waved them away with his sword. "Leave him be. Leave him be!" he cried. It was then that he noticed that many of the Outcasts were bandaged, that others lay stretched out under the trees. Marion was bending over one of the wounded.

"Oh, God, what has happened here?" Tuck said, suddenly alarmed. "Robin! Is Robin hurt?" cried Tuck. And much to his relief, he saw Robin parting the crowd to get to him. The two friends hugged each other.

"It's so good to have you back, Tuck," said Robin, and Tuck held him at arm's length, looking him up and down. "Not a scratch on me," Robin laughed. "Good as new."

"But there has been a fight, hasn't there? What happened?"

And Robin told him the whole story from the beginning, blow by blow. Friar Tuck listened in silence, his brow furrowing all the while in fury. "The Abbess of Kirkleigh, it could be no one else," he said. "I told you about her, the Sheriff's sister and Guy of Gisbourne's lover. Had I been here I would have known her. I would know her anywhere, fiendish witch that she is. Let me just come within a sword's length of her, by God's good grace." He shook his head. "I should have been here, I should have been here."

Only Marion seemed to be able to comfort him. "It's over, Tuck," she said. "What's done is done. Martin is safe, and the Sheriff and his men stay inside the walls of Nottingham, too frightened even to come out. Better still, you are back home, safe and well. We have missed you, Tuck. We did not think we would, but we did."

As the laughter died away, the young man whispered something into Tuck's ear. Tuck nodded and looked around anxiously. "Little John," said Tuck. "Where's Little John?" He grasped Robin by the arm. "He's not one of the thirty-five, tell me he's not."

"Don't worry. He's fine," said Robin. "He's gone back to the battlefield again, to collect the best of their swords. He won't be long."

And the young man smiled for the first time.

"You know Little John, do you?" Robin asked him.

"Oh, he knows him." Tuck spoke for him, and put his arm around the newcomer. "He knows him well. I tell you, this man is heaven sent, by God's good grace, heaven sent. Did we not pray every day for freedom and justice? Well, we will have them both, and soon, for God has heard us. This man is the answer to all our prayers. With his help we shall have our good King Richard back home where he belongs. We know the vile usurper, Prince John, scours the land for gold, claiming he needs it to pay the King's ransom. But we know, too, that the last thing in the world he wants is his brother back on the throne. Why else does Richard still languish in his Austrian dungeon after all this time? And was it not because of this that we collected the ransom ourselves and hid it away in our cave chapel, ready for the right moment? Now, by God's good grace, the right moment has come. We will pay the ransom and fetch back our King."

"But how? No one knows where the King is," said Robin.

Friar Tuck smiled. "This man does. Tell them, Blondel, my friend, how you found good King Richard, tell them how you did it." The young man hesitated, looking to Friar Tuck for reassurance. "Don't worry yourself. They're an ugly bunch, but not as savage as they look. Speak up. Tell them what you told me in Canterbury."

And so Blondel began. "I am Blondel. I am the King's minstrel. I was with him in the Holy Land. At the end of each day he always loved to hear me sing, and one song in particular he loved. It soothed him, he said, soothed away his worries and his pains. Sometimes we would sing it together. We called it 'The Candlelight Song,' a flickering tune like no other I have ever heard.

"He was taken hostage on his way home from the wars; and like everyone else, all I knew was that he was being held by the Duke of Austria, but I did not know where. The duke has dozens of castles. It could have been in any of them. So for these last months, I have wandered through Austria, playing the mad minstrel. I would walk around and around each castle, singing 'The Candlelight Song,' hoping he would hear me and know me and sing back the song. Castle after castle I tried, and there was no answering refrain. I began to despair.

"The day I found him was a wild and windy day. I remember that because I had to sing out loud against the wind. I thought it was an echo I was hearing at first, but it was not. It was another voice, but the same song. I had found my master." His voice caught in his throat at this moment, and his eyes filled with tears. "I could not see him, only his hands on the bars of the dungeon window across the moat, but it was his voice." He could speak no more.

"And do you know what Blondel did?" Friar Tuck took up the story. "He did what any loyal Englishman would have done, anyone who did not know our Prince John as we do. He came back to London and told Prince John where the King was being held. And what did our valiant Prince do? Did he send men to besiege the castle and rescue his brother? Did he send the ransom money? No. None of these. Tell them what he said, Blondel."

Blondel spoke through his tears. "He said that Richard could rot there, for all he cared." The crowd murmured with indignation.

"And then," Tuck went on expansively, "and then the miracle happened. By God's good grace, Blondel came to Canterbury, to the holy shrine, to pray for his master; and I was there at vespers, praying, too. I heard beside me a man crying, this man. We got to talking outside the shrine. We ate together, and I confess it, we drank together too, and he told me his story. It was God's good grace that brought us together, and it'll be God's good grace that will take us over the seas to Austria to pay the ransom and bring our King out of his captivity. He will have his master home, and we shall have our King back on his throne, and justice at last in this land." He turned to Robin and patted his great belly. "Well, and isn't it food time now, by God's good grace?"

Just then Little John came into the encampment laden with swords. He saw Blondel, dropped the swords with a clatter, and ran to him and swept him up in a great bear hug.

What a feast they had that night around the fire! Blondel taught the Outcasts "The Candlelight Song," and they sang it again and again until everyone knew it by heart.

As they sang, Robin planned. With Will Scarlett and his father and Marion and Little John and Much and Tuck, he devised how they might bring Richard safely back to Sherwood. All knew that there was no time to lose. The King could die in his dungeon. Prince John could pay the ransom before they did and have him murdered—he was capable even of fratricide, they had no doubt of that. They had to move fast.

The smelting of the gold began that night. It was to take all the next day for Little John to turn gold chains and plates and cups and ewers and crosses into golden horseshoes. After all, as Little John said himself, you couldn't be too careful with all these nasty folk about, thieving everything they could lay their filthy hands on. Nothing was safe these days; but safer than almost anything were horseshoes. No one ever stole horseshoes. And so that the golden horseshoes would not wear away, each horse would be doubly shod. A shoe of solid gold next to the horse's hoof, and an iron one over to protect it. Will Scarlett worked night and day at his cutting and stitching, until Robin and Much and Little John looked their parts—and that was no easy task. All three had to look like noblemen, like emissaries from the court of Prince John. They were to be accompanied by their holy friar, who insisted on a new habit of the best Irish cloth; and by Blondel, of course, who would travel as their servant and would therefore need no new clothes.

"I shall call myself Robin, Earl of Locksley. How does that sound?" said Robin, dressed up in his finery for the first time and parading like a peacock in front of Marion and little Martin that last evening.

Marion smiled at him a little ruefully. "Just don't ever forget who you really are," she said. "And come back safe to Sherwood, for me and for Martin."

And so, the next morning, they rode away, their horses' hooves glinting gold in the sunlight; but they were not glinting for long. By the time they reached the London road, the horses were covered in mud to their fetlocks. Behind them they left the band of Outcasts in the care of Marion, Will, and Robin's father, every one of them already longing for the day the travelers would return to Sherwood with their King.

They put up at an inn by the river at Southwark in London, a dingy, stinking place full of rats and filth that they were all glad to leave. The sea crossing was wretched, too, particularly for Robin. Heaving over the ship's side, he longed for the trees of Sherwood, and for ground that did not move under him. It was made all the worse for him because Little John would keep clapping him on the back and telling him to cheer up. Robin had never before felt like strangling him.

The roads through France were no better than in England. The early-autumn rains had turned them into quagmires. Every river they came to was swollen and bank-high. Fording was usually quite impossible, and there were often long

detours to the nearest bridge. Then they would lose their way. Tuck's much-vaunted perfect sense of direction was proved fallible on too many occasions.

Every morning and evening Little John checked the horses' golden shoes, all twenty of them, to be sure they were secure beneath the iron ones. Being of softer metal, they flattened out more than iron shoes, but they were tailor made to each hoof, and with a few new nails from time to time, they lasted well enough. Weary and saddlesore, they journeyed four long weeks before they reached Austria and the Danube. When at long last Blondel saw the castle rising from the valley floor in the bend of the river, their sense of elation and relief banished at once all thoughts of exhaustion. "That's the place," cried Blondel. "I have dreamed of it night and day."

At Robin's suggestion, Blondel set off at once alone, to find out if the King was still there. They watched him ride slowly around the castle again and again, before he came galloping back to them. He was breathless with excitement. "He's there, the King is there. I sang. He sang. He's there. I told him we had brought the ransom, that we were taking him home."

"Then what are we waiting for?" said Robin, settling his heels to his horse's side. And the five of them rode down into the valley, splashed though a stream at a canter, and thundered over the drawbridge into the castle courtyard.

Armed men rushed at them from every side. "We are from the court of Prince John of England," Robin cried, brushing aside the spear pointed at his chest. "We have come to pay King Richard's ransom, but we will pay it only when we see the King brought out alive and well."

"We will see your money first, Englishman," said a voice from the top of the steps. The soldiers backed away instantly. "I would not trust an Englishman as far as I could spit." And the man threw his cloak about him as he came down the steps toward them.

"And who are you to insult us so?" Robin asked.

"The Duke of Austria," the man replied. "And you?"

"He is Robin of Locksley," said Friar Tuck, dismounting slowly, "and I am his friar, and my bottom is sore."

"And where is the ransom? You have no baggage."

"These fine English horses," replied Robin, "are all the ransom you will get. They are worth at least a hundred thousand pounds, your price for our King, I believe."

"A joke." The Duke's hand was on his sword now. "A bad English joke."

At this, Friar Tuck stopped rubbing his bottom; and suddenly, before anyone

could stop him, his sword was in his hand, and he lunged toward the Duke, lifting his chin with its point.

"No joke," he snarled. "I'm not laughing, am I? Now, by God's good grace, you will do as I say, or I shall separate your dukely head from your dukely body."

The Duke of Austria waved back his men.

"Tell your soldiers to lay down their weapons," said Friar Tuck. And Little John and Much made quite sure that every one of them did.

"Now," said Robin. "Bring me Richard the Lionheart, and you shall have these horses, which are full payment of the ransom, as I have promised. You will see when you examine the horses that I do not break promises. In return, I shall want fresh horses, and your word on the Holy Bible that we shall be able to leave this castle and this country unhindered."

The Duke made the oath on Friar Tuck's Bible, and he gave the order for the King to be brought up. He had little choice, for Friar Tuck's sword was never far from his throat. So they waited there for the King, as the first snows of winter began to fall.

The man who stumbled, blinking, into the courtyard some minutes later looked more like a beggar than a king. Emaciated almost beyond recognition, he walked slowly, unsteadily, toward them over the cobbles. Little John ran to his side to support him.

The King looked up at him. "Little John." He smiled. And then Blondel was there, too, on his knee before his beloved King. "Dear friend," said the King, "how can I ever thank you?"

"Thank Robin Hood and his Outcasts, Sire," said Blondel. "It is they who have done this. I just pointed the way."

And so, in that cold courtyard, Tuck still guarding the Duke, and snowflakes falling all about them, Richard the Lionheart met Robin Hood.

"Sire," said Robin, "weak though I know you are, we must leave at once. Fresh horses are being brought. We leave these behind in payment of your ransom."

"Five horses for a king?" said the King. "Hardly a king's ransom, is it?"

Robin bent to lift one of their hooves. "Each one of their shoes is of solid gold, gold raised in Sherwood to bring you home. Can you believe it, Sire, but this goat of an Austrian duke thought we were trying to cheat him."

Fresh horses were being led into the courtyard now, saddled and ready. Little John and Blondel helped the King up into his saddle.

"Tuck," said Robin, "let the Duke have his ugly head. Onto your horse, and let's be off." And he strode over to the Duke of Austria, who was clutching his

throat, his face pale with fear. "All you have to do, my lord Duke, is to take the shoes off all our horses, and you will find your ransom paid in full. We have our King. You have your gold. Everyone is happy. You will not mind if I take your cloak for my King?"

"So you are Robin Hood," said the Duke, taking off his cloak and handing it to Robin. "I have heard of you, and know you to be a loyal and an honorable man. Your King does not deserve you, as you will one day find out."

They were words Robin could not get out of his head as the men rode out from the castle.

Every day they traveled, every meal they ate, every night they slept, the King grew in strength. At night he would sit by the fire and tell them of his crusades to the Holy Land; of the battles he had won, the castles he had besieged; of his enemy, Saladin, of whom he spoke with more respect and even affection than his allies. They heard of the treachery of the Duke of Austria, and how the other crusading kings and princes quarreled endlessly among themselves. He would not rest, he said, until Jerusalem was in Christian hands again. Then Blondel would sing, and Richard would sing, and they would all sing.

The King had scarcely been in England over the last ten years, and as they rode he quizzed them endlessly on the state of his kingdom. They told him of the injustices imposed on the people by Prince John and his sheriffs up and down the land; of the Sheriff of Nottingham in particular, and Sir Guy of Gisbourne, and how the two of them drove the people from their homes; of the starvation and deep poverty, of the torture and mutilation all done in the King's name. And when alone with the King, Blondel spoke of all the good that Robin and his band of Outcasts had done.

The King listened to them all, but even while he was listening he seemed restless, looking past them or through them as they spoke. He would deal with the

Sheriff of Nottingham on his return, and Sir Guy of Gisbourne, too; that much he did promise them. Such terrible deeds could not and would not go unpunished; but Richard's brother was his brother, and though he acknowledged John was weak, he would hear no more against him.

The crossing was calm this time, to Robin's great relief; but he stayed out on deck—he felt better that way. On the last morning at sea, the King joined him there. "As soon as I can, Robin," he said, "I will come to Sherwood. I owe you that, and much more besides. I shall see to it that your Outcasts are free again. Their virtue and their courage will have reward, have no fear. And the Sheriff of Nottingham and Sir Guy of Gisbourne will have their just deserts, I promise you." He gazed out toward the white cliffs of Dover and sighed deeply. "I was not born a king, Robin. Had he lived, my older brother would have been king in my place. I did not want the crown. I am a soldier, never happier than in a fight; and no cause is more dear to me than the capture of Jerusalem. How else does a soldier find his way to heaven, unless he fights for God? I was not made for a comfortable court, for the niceties of diplomacy, or the machinations of ambitious ministers and counselors."

"But your people," said Robin, "they need you at home."

The King shook his head. "No, they need people like you, Robin. You should have been born King, not me." And he walked away.

It was the dawn of Christmas Day when they arrived at last in London and rode through the silent streets up to the Tower. The guard at the gate stood staring openmouthed.

"I am no ghost, man. I am your King. Have the gate opened and send for my brother. He'll be in bed. He always was a late riser."

Sitting on his throne with Blondel at his feet, Richard the Lionheart waited for his brother in silence. On one side of him stood Robin and Much, on the other Little John and Friar Tuck. They heard doors opening and closing upstairs, urgent whisperings, running feet; and then they saw the solitary figure of Prince John on the staircase, wrapping himself in a sable-trimmed gown.

"Come on down, John," said the King. "I shall not eat you. And neither will Robin Hood, though he has cause enough, I believe.

"I am home again, brother John, the ransom paid. What, are you not glad to see me? I have come home to wish you a merry Christmas. Don't worry, I will not stay for long this time, for I have business in Sherwood Forest, urgent business that cannot wait. Don't stand there gaping. Come and embrace your brother, John; or should I call you Judas?"

TEN

REVENGE IS SWEET

 All this while, in Nottingham Castle Sir Guy of Gisbourne and the Abbess of Kirkleigh had been searching for some sure way of destroying Robin Hood and the Outcasts; but neither plotting nor prayers had come up with anything. Many of their own spies had deserted and joined the Outcasts. Bribery proved fruitless too. They doubled the price on Robin's head, but still no one came forward. As for the Sheriff, he sat glowering in his castle, terrified of every creaking door, and seeing devils and portents in every flitting bat or screeching owl.

The three of them were huddled close to the fire that Christmas night, the wind whining and moaning in the chimney. All of them were brooding darkly about the same thing, the same man.

Yet another Christmas had come and gone, and Robin Hood still lived. In his fury and frustration, Sir Guy of Gisbourne kicked out at a sprig of holly and sent it flying into the red heat of the fire, where it crackled, roared, and then vanished in a shower of sparks up the chimney.

Behind them, his eyes shining in the darkness at the back of the room, stood a servant holding an ewer of wine, a trusted servant; but, unknown to them, now an Outcast and a spy.

"Numbskulls," said the Abbess suddenly. "We have been numbskulls. May I burn in hellfire if I have not found the perfect way! We'll smoke them out, brother. We'll burn Sherwood around their ears, burn it to the ground so there's nowhere left for them to hide."

"But you can't," the Sheriff protested. "It's the King's forest."

"The King, dear brother, is hundreds of miles away in an Austrian dungeon, is he not? For God's sake, he's very probably dead and buried by now. And besides, brother, you speak for the King in Nottingham, so you *are* the King in Nottingham."

"It could work," said Sir Guy of Gisbourne, springing to his feet. "It could really work. We wait for a wind from the west. We have all our men, every one of them, ready and waiting on the east side of the forest. We light the fire, and the rats run straight into our trap. It's so simple, so beautiful."

All through the night of New Year's Eve, hundreds of the Sheriff's men lay in wait along the eastern edge of Sherwood, every quiver full, every sword and spear and ax sharpened for the kill. Hidden in the woods behind them, the Sheriff's horsemen waited and watched. Nothing had been left to chance. Not a single Outcast was to be left alive.

In the gray dark of predawn, with just a dozen men, the Sheriff and Sir Guy rode out of Nottingham, torches in hand. The wind was gusting from the west, and the forest was dry from weeks of frost. It would burn like the sprig of holly.

They timed it to the minute, reaching the forest just as the dawn was breaking.

"We have him now," said the Sheriff, riding forward with his blazing torch.

As he spoke, a shadow moved and stepped out from the trees. The shadow spoke and became Robin Hood. "Drop the torch, my lord. I have an arrow pointing at your heart, my lord Sheriff."

The Sheriff did not hesitate, but threw down the torch at Robin's feet. Then there were other shadows flitting through the trees, dozens, hundreds of them. All the Sheriff's men but one threw down their torches at once. With a scream of rage, Sir Guy of Gisbourne charged his horse toward the nearest tree. He threw himself flat along the neck of his horse, the torch thrust out ahead of him like a lance.

Robin wheeled around as the Sheriff passed, and he let loose his arrow. It took Sir Guy of Gisbourne through the neck and lifted him clean from the saddle. He was dead before he hit the ground.

When the body was still at last, the Sheriff looked up. The man standing before him was not dressed like Robin and the others, in Lincoln green. His red cloak bore on it the crest of the three golden lions rampant, the arms of the King of England, of King Richard the Lionheart. He recognized the face now, and from that moment he knew he was going to die. He was hauled unceremoniously from his horse and thrown down before the King.

"Have mercy, Sire," he begged, grasping the King's feet.

"Once before, you were shown mercy," said the King. "Never again. These last few days I have lived with the Outcasts. I have heard each of their stories. I go to fight a holy war for God and country, and while I am gone, men like you play the petty tyrant. You thieve from the people, you pillage, you corrupt, and you do it in my name, too. You were going to burn down my forest and massacre those brave few so despised by you, so maltreated. The Holy Book says, 'Ye reap what ye sow.' Within the hour you shall hang by the neck like the common criminal you are.

Not a man, not a woman, not a child, in this company, nor in this world, I think, will mourn your death. Take him to the gibbet."

Much, the miller's son, stepped forward. "It was promised to me, Sire," he said. "Robin Hood promised me his death."

"Then he is yours," replied the King.

The King and the Outcasts stood at the edge of Sherwood and watched as Much led the whimpering Sheriff away, down into the valley where the gibbet stood waiting.

Suddenly the sky darkened overhead as, from all over Sherwood, it seemed, the crows gathered.

"Anything you want," pleaded the Sheriff. "Please let me live. I have gold, more gold than the King himself." Much made no reply, to this or to any other of his entreaties, but fixed the rope quickly about the Sheriff's neck and hanged him high.

Only when he was dead, with his legs swinging in the wind, did Much speak at last. "For my father," he said.

As the Outcasts passed by the gibbet on their way into Nottingham that morning, every one of them looked their last on the hated Sheriff of Nottingham; and terrible though the sight was, it stirred no pity in their hearts. When the

people of the city came out to greet their King, and when the Outcasts were cheered all through the streets from every doorstep, from every window, they could not help but feel sad that at the moment of their greatest triumph, a golden time of great comradeship was coming to an end. Nothing would ever be quite the same again.

But spirits rose again that night as they all feasted together in the great hall of Nottingham Castle, Robin and Marion on either side of King Richard. Friar Tuck blessed the venison and then ate most of it himself, so the King said. Much wrestled against all comers and won every time, as everyone knew he would. Blondel sang for them, and as the castle rang to the sweet sound of "The Candlelight Song," the people in the streets of Nottingham outside heard it and danced with joy. For them, as well as for the Outcasts, the cruel days, the dark days, were over at last.

Out in the moonlit countryside, far beyond the city walls, there was no such happiness. The sound of distant revelry was a bitter accompaniment to the Abbess of Kirkleigh as she cut down the Sheriff from the gibbet and with her sisters laid him alongside Sir Guy of Gisbourne in a cart. The Sheriff's army had simply drifted away and vanished. She had no hope left, only hate.

She lifted her face to the full moon. "Hear me, Robin Hood," she screeched. "For what you have done today, you shall pay with your life. Here lie my brother, and the only man I have loved on this earth. For their deaths, you will die, I swear it."

That same night, the two men were buried at Kirkleigh in the abbey graveyard, and even as the sisters were filling in their graves the Abbess was upstairs in her room praying; and when she prayed now, it was not to God but to the devil. "Deliver Robin Hood up to me," she hissed, "and I am yours for life."

The King did not stay long in Nottingham, just long enough to decree that all Outcasts should live and work where they pleased, like other men and women; that all property, houses, lands, goods, and chattels should be restored to their rightful owners, and proper restitution made from the Sheriff's own fortune.

"And lastly," he declared, "I decree that in recognition of their courageous resistance to the recent tyrannies, Robin Hood and his Outcasts shall be able to hunt through the Royal Forest of Sherwood for the rest of their lives."

There was much rapturous cheering at this, and banging of tables. But the King had not finished. "However," he went on, "for this consideration I want to borrow your leader, only for a while. I want Robin Hood to act as counselor to me when I return to London. I have much need of men about me that I can trust. Well, Robin, will you come?"

Robin was flattered, but he did not want to go. Home had always been the forest. He wanted nothing else, to be nowhere else. He and Marion had always dreamed of living and farming on the edge of Sherwood, in the same house, the same land where he had grown up as a boy. But the King had asked him, and he could not refuse. "I come with my friends and my family, Sire, or not at all," he said.

"Agreed," replied the King, and the two men embraced.

But the hall had fallen stonily silent.

"No!" cried one of the Outcasts. "Stay with us, Robin." And the cry echoed around the hall, the Outcasts all on their feet in protest.

Robin did all he could to appease them. "I'll be back," he said. "As Tuck would say it—by God's good grace, I'll be back."

But the joy had gone suddenly out of the feast.

"How could I say no to him?" said Robin later, when he and Marion were alone.

"You could not," she replied. "But how I wish he had not asked!"

So it was with heavy hearts that they left the next day for London, Robin alongside the King; little Martin on Robin's saddle, clinging to the pommel; and behind them Blondel and Much and Tuck and Little John and Marion, leading his

father. But as they rode through the marketplace, the Outcasts surrounded them and would not let them pass.

Will Scarlett spoke up, as he had done all those years before when Robin had first met them. "May God keep you, good Robin," he said. "And may he bring you and yours back safe and sound." Will looked suddenly old and frail, and Robin knew then he should not be leaving him, nor any of the Outcasts. But there was no turning back.

"Take care, Will," he said, and the crowd parted reluctantly and watched him leave, their eyes filled with tears.

Robin had thought that in London he would pine for the open skies, for the trees, but he did not. He and his family lacked for nothing; they had the best food, servants, fine clothes. Their house was warm. There were those Londoners at first who mocked their country ways and country talk, but never more than once. And when it was learned who they were, they were fêted like royalty themselves.

Marion saw at once that Robin was liking the attention far too much for his own good, but she said nothing, hoping that the newness of it all would soon wear off. Unlike Robin, she longed for the simplicities of Sherwood.

On the banks of the Thames, Robin and his father taught the King's bowmen how to split a wand at a hundred paces. And Much saw to it that every soldier was fit in wind and limb, for he was a hard taskmaster. Little John busied himself in the King's armory, so they saw little of him these days. As for Tuck, they hardly saw him at all. Time lay heavily on him, and he seemed to be spending most of his time in the taverns.

The King called his council together each week, but Robin soon saw that there was little point in his being there. The King talked of nothing but his next crusade. He seemed completely disinterested in anything that did not serve that single purpose. He needed two thousand more good men. He wanted Robin to recruit them and train them. He needed to raise taxes for the campaign.

"But the people have been taxed enough for foreign wars, Sire," Robin said. "They need their King at home."

Richard smiled at him, but there was an edge to his tone. "You stick to what you're good at, Robin," he said. "Find me soldiers. Train them as well as you trained your Outcasts, that's all I ask."

And Robin did as he was asked, although he was beginning to wonder why his advice on all other matters was so often ignored.

Among his soldiers, among the people of London, he was a hero; he was Robin of Sherwood, he was a legend. His exploits in Sherwood and his rescue of the King were the talk of the taverns. Among the courtiers, though, he was just a dressed-up common forester with a white-haired cagot for a wife; but all the same a man to beware of and to flatter, for they knew he was as close to the King as anyone. So wherever he went, in court or out of it, he was fawned on and lionized.

Marion looked on helpless as Robin changed before her eyes. His fame and fortune were going to his head and he did not seem even to notice it. He was beginning to believe in the legend.

She confided her fears to Robin's father. "I am losing him," she said. "He's never home. Something is always more important, even than little Martin."

But Robin's father could be of little comfort to her. He, too, no longer knew his own son. "He does not listen to me anymore, nor to anyone but the King," he said. "He treats his faithful Much as if he is not there. He leaves poor Tuck to drink himself into a stupor in the taverns, and always his mind seems to be elsewhere. If we could only go home to Sherwood, then he would find himself again, I know he would."

One night Robin came bursting in even later than usual. Marion and his father were sitting before the fire. He could not contain himself. "You'll never guess!" he cried. "I am to be made a knight. Robin Hood, Outcast and outlaw, is to be made a knight. What do you think of that? Tomorrow I shall be Sir Robin of Locksley— the King let me choose my title. And you shall be my Lady Marion."

Marion looked him straight in the eye as she spoke. "Never, Robin, never, as long as I live. I am no lady. I am Marion, mother of our child, and your companion in life. I have stayed long enough in this place. It is too comfortable and full of sycophants and title seekers. There is corruption in the very air we breathe. Tomorrow I shall go home to Sherwood, and I shall take little Martin with me. We do not belong here."

"But why?" asked Robin, unable to believe what he was hearing.

"I was the wife of Robin Hood, a fair man, a kind man, a thinking man who sought only good for others, who loved his friends and was loved by them. Now he has become someone else, someone I cannot love, cannot live with."

"I, too, will go home, Robin," said his father, "home to Sherwood, where we all belong. We are fish out of water here. See what has become of Tuck. See what has become of you. Listen to us, Robin. Come with us now, before it is too late."

"But I can't. The King . . ."

"The King! The King! Always the King!" Marion cried. "The King is not God, Robin. Have you forgotten that? Have you forgotten yourself entirely?"

And Robin knew then that he had, but his pride would not let him say so. "I stay with my King," he said, turning away. "You go if you like."

ELEVEN

DEADLY NIGHTSHADE

At dawn the next day Marion and little Martin and Robin's father made ready to leave. Much was there to help them. "Take care of him, Much," said Marion as she mounted her horse. "And bring him back to Sherwood when he's himself again. Bring him home safe."

"I should come with you," said Much, lifting up little Martin and setting him astride the saddle in front of her. "But I cannot abandon him."

"I know that," Marion said, and she leaned down and kissed him. "Tell him I love him and I'll be waiting for him in Sherwood. I have left him the silver arrow. He'll know why. Don't let him lose it."

From an upper window, Robin watched them leave, but he could not bring himself to go down to say good-bye. As they rode away he lifted the silver arrow and waved it, but none of them saw it.

When they had gone, Much came into his room and found Robin sitting on his bed and crying like a child. The silver arrow lay on his lap. "You're a fool, Robin Hood," said Much.

"I know it," replied Robin. "I know it."

King Richard knighted him that same day, in the river meadow where the bowmen trained. But even as the blade rested on his shoulder, Robin felt no pleasure in it, no pride, only a deep longing for Marion and for Sherwood.

The entire court was there, Prince John with them, looking sour as usual. Two thousand bowmen waved their bows and cheered Robin as he rose to his feet to be embraced by the King. He saw Much and Little John standing some way off, but in their eyes there was nothing but disappointment. He looked everywhere for Tuck but could see him nowhere.

The King held him at arm's length. "Well, Sir Robin of Locksley," he began, "you have come a long, long way from your woods. And you shall go farther too. I leave on my crusade in two weeks, if the winds are fair. Come with me as my

captain, Robin. With you beside me, we shall defeat Saladin and we shall march together through the gates of Jerusalem."

"And your own kingdom, Sire?" said Robin. "What becomes of your kingdom while you are gone?"

"My brother, John, will manage without me. He has learned his lesson—have you not, brother?"

And Prince John looked down at his feet and said nothing.

"Do we ever learn our lessons, I wonder, before it is too late, Sire?" said Robin. "I belong here. I belong in England."

"So you will not come?" The King was suddenly angry.

"No, Sire, I will stay at home and guard your kingdom for you while you are gone. When a shepherd leaves his sheep, Sire, he does not leave them unguarded."

"And I stay, too, Sire," said Little John. "I have made you all the swords you need for your crusade. Where Robin is, I must be."

"Then go back to your woods, for all I care," cried the King. "I shall take Jerusalem without you." And he turned on his heel and walked away.

It took all that day for the three of them to find Tuck. Little John knew most of his drinking haunts, but he was not to be found in any of them. Then one tavern keeper, who knew Tuck well, told them that he had left this tavern two days before, saying he had finished with drink forever, that from then on he would be praying his way back to God. So they searched every church and chapel in London and found him at last kneeling before the altar of St. Bartholomew the Great, in Smithfield.

When Tuck looked up and saw them, he covered his face with his hands and wept. "Take me home, boys," he said. "Take me home."

They set off at first light and rode north all day without stopping, making over forty miles by nightfall. Even so they had not caught up with Marion and Robin's father, as they had expected. "They cannot be far ahead of us now," said Little John. "But if we ride at night we may ride past them without knowing it. Let's find somewhere to sleep. We'll start out again early tomorrow morning. We'll catch up with them soon enough."

There were no inns nearby, nor monasteries or priories, so they made camp in a wood and ate together around a fire, as they had done so often before. It was a damp and foggy night, and they lay huddled close to the fire for warmth; but despite all they could do, Tuck would not stop shivering. By morning he had a fever and Much had to help him onto his horse. Slumped and silent in his saddle, Tuck rode on uncomplaining all through the next day and the next, but they had to go at a walk now. And still there was no sign of Marion and the others on the road.

Heavy rain and a fierce, whipping wind forced them to stop early on the third day. Tuck was coughing almost continuously by this time, and Robin knew that to go on would be the death of him. He needed rest. He needed a doctor. So when they came to a nunnery on the outskirts of a small village, they hammered on the door and asked for shelter, for help.

The nuns took them in and did all they could. For two nights and two days, Tuck tossed and turned in his fever, close to death. They bled him with leeches, but that did not help. They bathed him in cold water to cool him, but that only seemed to make him worse. The nuns worked tirelessly, but Tuck sank into a deep sleep and would not wake. His breathing became shallow and rasping. Much and Little John and Robin sat by his bed, praying and waiting for the end.

One of the nuns came in to pray with them. As she was about to leave the room, she said, "I don't know much about these things, and I don't want to raise false hopes; but I do know of someone, an Abbess, a healer, who lives nearby. She has been known to heal when all other remedies have failed."

"Then send for her!" cried Robin. "And hurry, please hurry."

That evening, an unseen face peered through the grill of the cell where Tuck lay surrounded by his companions, all on their knees and praying. The face smiled, but it was a cold and venomous smile. Then the face vanished.

The same nun brought their supper to the cell, leek soup. "The Abbess. The healer," said Robin. "Where is she? Will she be long?"

"In the kitchens," replied the nun, "preparing a medicine for him. She won't be long. You should eat your soup; it'll give you strength. And besides, all waste is wicked in the Lord's eyes." And with that, she left.

Little John tried the soup first. It was good and peppery, he said. Robin ate it, more to warm himself than anything else, for his feet were frozen. Only Much refused it. He sat closest to Tuck, his eyes never leaving Tuck's face, not for an instant. Minutes later the door opened and the nun was there again.

"I have the good friar's medicine," she said, "and the Abbess said I was to pour it down his throat. I will need you to lift him for me, or else he may choke."

"But if she has not seen him," Robin asked, "how does she know what to give him?"

"I asked her the same thing," replied the nun. "She says it is a universal remedy; and she is a holy woman. We must have faith." And with Much holding Tuck in his arms, she poured the medicine into Tuck's mouth and wiped his lips afterward. "He's in God's hands now," she said, crossing herself. And then she left them.

She had been gone only a few moments when Robin began to feel his head swirling, a pain gripping his stomach, and a sickly taste in his mouth that reminded him of the terrible sea voyage he had made. He clutched at the bed to stop himself from falling, but he could not.

When he opened his eyes he saw Little John crawling beside him on the floor. John was reaching out toward him, his face contorted with pain, his eyes wide with fear.

"The soup," whispered Little John. "We are poisoned. We are dead men." And Robin felt the first shudder of death come over him, and he knew it, too.

Much was bending over him, trying to lift him. "Help me up, Much," said Robin. "I want to see trees once more before I die. And I will die standing, looking my God in the face." He stood by the window, looking out, the color draining from his cheeks. He leaned back on Much and looked his last at the trees and the sky. "The Abbess. It was the Abbess. I should have known. Too late, too late. The Abbess of Kirkleigh, it could be no one else. She has done us in, Much. You did not eat your soup, did you?"

"No, Robin."

"Dear Much. Always wise," Robin breathed. "Wise and silent. Give me my bow now, and Marion's silver arrow. I shall shoot one last time through this window, and where this arrow lies, there you must bury us. Tell her I am sorry, and that I love her. Care for my family as you have cared for me."

He had not the strength to draw the bow himself; but with Much's help, he lifted it, felt his thumb knuckle touch his nose, looked along the arrow to its silver tip, and let fly. He never saw where it landed, for he was dead.

Much, the miller's son, laid Robin in his grave the next morning, his horn, his bow, and his silver arrow beside him. And on either side of him, Much dug two other graves, one for Little John and one for Friar Tuck. Above each he placed a

cross of English oak, but with no inscription, for Much could not write. The nuns sang over them, blessed them, and wished them to heaven. Then the mourners left them where they lay.

As Much was about to leave, a rust red squirrel ran along a branch above him and dropped a nut at his feet, an acorn. He planted it in the soft, cold earth of Robin's grave. "So I'll always know where to find you, Robin," he said. "I have to go now, back to Sherwood; but first to Kirkleigh."

He was there by noon, and waiting in the shadows of the cloisters. The Abbess, still exulting, did not see him until he stepped out in front of her. Then she knew him at once, and what he had come for. She tried to escape but Much held her fast. "You ate deadly nightshade and you lived!" she cried.

"You killed the best heart in all England," said Much. "But I will not kill you here in this holy place, nor will you ever lie in sanctified ground. You lived for the devil and now you can go to him."

He took her far away from the abbey and hanged her from a wych elm tree, then buried her deep in the corner of a field of stubble where no one would ever find her and where her body would not taint the wheat.

By the time Much came to Sherwood again, there was snow on the ground. He found the house on the edge of the forest, saw the smoke rising from the chimney, saw little Martin pottering by the door with Robin's father, and Marion chopping wood. For weeks Much lived out in the cold, keeping watch over them but never wanting to make himself known, for he knew what news he would have to tell her.

In the end, it was she who found him. She was out hunting early one morning, stalking a deer, when she came across him crouching over a dying fire. He looked into her eyes, unable to speak.

"I know," she said. "I have known for weeks. If he was alive he'd have come home. I know he would." She held out her hands to him. "Did he tell you to look after us?" she asked, smiling. "I thought so. Then come with me, Much, and do as he says." They walked a little while together in silence. "Never tell me how it happened," she said, taking his arm. "It's in life I want to remember him, not in death."

When I woke I found myself on my side in the mud, and cold; and in my hand, still tightly grasped, the silver arrowhead. A jay had cackled somewhere nearby and brought me to my senses.

I sat up and remembered. I remembered the hurricane of the night before, sheltering with Gran under the stairs, the roe deer by the stream. But it all seemed to have happened such a long time ago, a lifetime ago.

I saw about me the devastated forest and my tree, my poor dead tree. And there were the bones in the earth beside me, and the skull I had dropped, the cow's horn, and the long curved stick. I knew there was more, much more, that I should remember, but I could not. I felt there was an echo of a dream inside me but that it was unreachable now and always would be.

I struggled to my feet and looked about me. God only knew how long I had been there. Clouds were scudding across the sky, chasing away the storm. It felt like midday. Gran would be out of her mind with worry. I had to get back.

I buried the bones where I had found them, scooping the earth over them hurriedly, and left. I took the horn and the silver arrowhead and the long curved stick with me—it seemed a pity to just bury them. I would take them home and clean them up. Maybe, I thought, maybe I could take them to the British Museum and find out how old they were. I would come back later and fill in the crater properly, so that no one would ever find the bones. It was my tree, so they were my bones. Later, though; I would do it all later.

I was halfway down the hill when I saw the berries. There were a dozen or more, black and as big as cherries. I felt suddenly hungry. I filled my hand with them and walked on. But for the cow's horn and the stick and the arrowhead, I would have eaten them there and then; but I hadn't a hand free to do it. Anyway, they would be good in yogurt with a lot of sugar on top. I would save them and have a feast when I got home. I hurried on, dropping one or two of the berries as I went.

I hid my treasures away in the back of the garage before I went in. I said I was sorry I had been gone so long, but Gran said she didn't know what I was talking about, that I had only been gone half an hour at the most. She rolled the berries from hand to hand, smelled them, and looked at me anxiously over her glasses. "You haven't eaten any of these, have you?" she asked.

"No," I said.

She took a deep breath. "Well, thank goodness for that. This is deadly nightshade. *Atropa belladonna.* Poisonous, deadly poisonous. You'd better wash your hands—and the rest of you while you're at it. Lord, you're a mess. Mud all over you. Look at you. What you need is a good bath. Upstairs."

I washed everything in the tub, my hands first, then my treasures. There was a lot of mud in the bathtub by the time I had finished. So I drained the water and ran another bath. Then Gran called upstairs and told me to turn it off, that with the electricity off, all the hot water we were going to get for a while was in the tank; and what was I doing having two baths anyway? So I washed the rest of me in the sink and scrubbed my treasures until they were as clean as I could get them. I stuck my tongue out at my reflection in the mirror.

"Idiot," I said. "You could have killed yourself."

Once in my bedroom, I hid away all my treasures, the stick behind my cupboard, the arrowhead and the cow's horn under my shirts in my chest of drawers.

Every day after that I took a spade and went back to the woods to fill in the crater left by my tree. It was a mammoth task of shoveling and hacking and shoveling again, but after a week or so I had filled it right in and stamped it down. I was sure now that no one would ever find the bones again. They were safe, safe from the timbermen who would, no doubt, soon be moving in with their heavy machinery; and safe from grave robbers.

But the bones would not leave me alone. Night after night I lay there and could think of nothing else. Something was unfinished, not right. The bones would not let me sleep. On one such sleepless night when Gran had gone up to bed and the house was quiet, I got up and spread my treasures out on my coverlet in the moonlight. That was when I thought of it. *I* was the grave robber.

My treasures had to go back. Then the bones would let me sleep.

It was a starry night, crisp and cold. I pulled my coat on over my bathrobe, stepped barefoot into my boots, and fetched the shovel. The stream runs louder at night. It was all I heard as I ran through the woods, back to where my tree lay, its bark covered in frost. I dug deep and buried them together, the stick, the horn,

and the arrowhead. I covered them and left quickly, before I could change my mind.

I stopped because I heard something that was not the stream. The trees seemed to be whispering in the wind. But there were no trees, and there was no wind.

"Son of Marion," came the whisper again, "son of Robin. God bless. God bless." And then I remembered my dream, every bit of it, and I have never again forgotten it.

I have never forgotten the place either, but I might have, had I not planted the acorn. It was an acorn from my tree, from Robin's tree. I cleared a space over his grave, as Much the miller's son had done before me. I nurtured the green shoot into a young oak sapling. I let no seed grown nearby. I let no other tree take its light.

Five years on, and it's twice my height already. Five hundred years on, and it'll be the most magnificent tree in the whole forest, just as it always was. Robin will like that. I know he will.